WHAT DID YOU DO IN THE WAR, GRANDAD?

The author has made every effort to ensure accuracy in the compiling of these memoirs and has gone to great lengths to try to ensure that locations, specialist naval terms and slang words used are spelled correctly. If any spelling or grammatical errors remain in the text, please accept the apologies of the author and the team that worked on the creation and editing of the book.

Every effort has been made to ensure that the use of photographs and maps in this book does not infringe the copyright of other people or organisations but where this has not been possible and amendments are required. Please contact the publisher who will be pleased to make any alterations necessary.

Some of the images in this book were given to the author and every effort has been made to obtain permission, but many of the people are no longer alive

Maps are ©OpenStreetMaps Contributors unless otherwise stated

Printed in the United Kingdom

First Printing, 2014

First Published 2014 by Appin Press, an imprint of Countyvise Ltd
14 Appin Road, Birkenhead, CH41 9HH

British Library Cataloguing in Publication Data.
A catalogue record for this book is available from the British Library.

ISBN 978-1-906823-92-4

Dedication

I would like to dedicate this book to my loving family for making me realise that what I had written was worth all the effort.

Contents

1

CALL UP

To fully understand the transformation from civilian life into service life is immensely difficult. To suddenly have to cast off the security of family life to a regimented daily existence, which required you to respond to loud broadcasts on a tannoy system or, the blast of a bugle, is not easy. To become like everyone else around you, with the same outlook, to tune your reactions to the way most others are thinking and behaving is sometimes devastatingly difficult.

My earliest impression in the Navy was that everyone was avoiding the necessity of doing anything that related in any way, shape or form, to work! Keep your head down and let it all wash over you unscathed, seemed to be the way to be.

To become inactive, even though you were now on what is called "active service".

Nevertheless, whatever other skills I was to accumulate later, the Royal Navy taught me three things;-

1) How to clean my shoes properly - for which to this day I am grateful.

2) How to read the Morse code, which I confess has not been of great commercial value, in this world of computer technology.

3) How to recognise at the early stage, anything that could even remotely resemble physical or mental exertion i.e. work!

On leaving the Navy at the tender age of twenty-four, I was worldly wise, well conserved and a total idle 'jack of no trade whatsoever'. I had been robbed of six of the most formative years in anyone's life.

Before expanding on the astonishingly uneventful career of the volunteer reservist, who stood behind, well behind, the real serviceman referred to above, it would be of interest to record how such a mistake was made to "volunteer" in the first place and secondly to examine the motives which lay behind such an unusual, unwise and ill considered error of judgement.

Lower deck law dictates that "you never volunteer for 'anyfink'". One must remember that various strata of human activity exist and that they are often worlds apart. Civilians usually had no concept of life in the services, armed or otherwise and service personnel, real service personnel, born and raised in those barrack-like cells known as married quarters; schooled by instructors (rather than parents, teachers); trained aboard institutions, such as training ship 'Arethusa', and 'finally finished off' at shore based establishments, such as HMS 'this' or 'that', had no idea whatsoever, what civilised or even notional living was all about.

Hence there is some excuse for a civilian father (having experienced as well as seen, real army activity on the Somme and Ypres during the disturbance of 1914 – 1918) giving his son the following benefit of his advice:

(1) Avoid the Air Force - "What goes up must come down."

(2) Avoid the Army -"You're cannon fodder."

(3) "Join the Navy - at least you can rely on three square meals a day and a dry bed - until the ship goes down!"

This was not very patriotic advice or very reassuring, but a real canny summing up by the Scottish father, anxious that the expense of raising his first born son would not be wasted unnecessarily.

So, stirred by common sense, and in the face of the certain inevitability of war becoming a fact, (because the politicians were saying just the opposite - Mr Chamberlain was waving a piece of fragile tissue from the top of an airline doorway, just back from seeing Adolf Hitler in Munich), this brave British son mounted the gangplank which leads to the deck of *HMS President*, moored still to this day on the Thames embankment. The ship housed the HQ of the London Division of The Wavy Navy, the ROYAL NAVAL VOLUNTEER RESERVE. This organisation has long been defunct, but I am the proud owner of the Long Service RNVR medal. Engraved all around its circumference with "YEOMAN OF SIGNALS A.D. BRUCE LD9/X 5232"

I was accompanied on this particular week night even by a good friend, who had promised to use his influence to "get me in". Jack Crosby had actually, back in 1937, enjoyed two weeks at sea, with the fleet on their summer manoeuvres. Jack being a full blooded healthy male, it takes little imagination to understand why, and still less need to describe these manoeuvres. Suffice to say they had little enough to do with the sea! In later years I was to comprehend that the only romance attached to the sea was upon the first sighting of land. There were never truer words written than those penned by Irving Berlin "it ain't what it's cracked up to be."

So I joined up without much difficulty or much excitement as I remember now. The medical folk were favourably impressed. At least I was still warm!

"YOU'RE IN"

My first impression was general cleanliness and well polished decks, cleared for action. Brasses also were very well polished particularly a brass bust of a maidenly figure-head which often graced the bow of sailing ships. This one was a of a very generously breasted, ample proportioned female form which had attracted great loving tender care, as it stood on its pedestal. Some sailor's hands, being very fond of the arts, must have lavished tremendous attention to the arts for posterity. His zeal and his cleavage to his duties were to be admired. Regular and undivided (if you will forgive an inappropriate word) attention had been applied to his polishing duties. No such other trophy had ever received such loving and heart-felt caresses.

The ensuing months were rather boring, for it appeared that the navy didn't really want me to enhance their reputation after all. War was being planned. Trenches were being dug in Hyde Park and some of the rich were preparing to leave for more acceptable "climates." I felt beyond the reach of those "four feathered 'psychos'" but no one knew, and even fewer could see, that I was not in uniform simply because I had not as yet been issued with one! I had been a reservist since the autumn of 1938 and went off to war on 21st September 1939 still wearing civvies gear.

I carried on my new found profession as a "By-Hand Boy" for a well known West End estate agency. My responsibilities were a sort of 'Wells Fargo' job, to take messages, letters, packages etc. "by hand", but on foot, to various London addresses, mostly in the city.

The Bus fare from Pall Mall/Haymarket to the Bank of England was 3d! My weekly wage for this absorbing work, was 15/- (Fifteen shillings) or 75p, per week of $5^{1/2}$ days. We had to work on Saturdays until 1 o'clock. My London Underground tube season ticket cost five shillings, - the rest I lavished on my girlfriend, Joan! My father ruled that whenever you gained your very first paid job, you were allowed to keep it all and not contribute to the family budget. I did not hire the Albert Hall to celebrate my new found wealth!

What I really wanted was to show off my uniform. I wanted to flash my call up papers around the office to the ooh's and aahs of the silk stocking'd bevy of girls in the typing pool. The frustration of having neither uniform nor call-up papers was short lived. War came as an interesting distraction. Those packages would have to be carried by someone more junior, less reliable, but maybe I had to attend to the King's pleasure, with far more important and dangerous work to carry through. His Majesty's Royal Britannic Navy was about to call me to the colours, because it needed me; the war was about to begin in earnest!

After the first three weeks of declared war, during which time little change could be detected in almost anyone's lifestyle, I began to get impatient. I felt "neglected" by the Sea Lords. Surely they knew what they were doing? (What an assumption to make about any Lords - let alone those with salt in their veins). But why was Errol Flynn, the film star, apparently doing everything? Here was a perfectly fit, fresh and fine specimen of British manhood, of proud Scottish descent, waiting on the side lines to grace the name of future battle honours and steam into action with torpedoes blasting in all directions at once!

2

CIVVIES TO SERVICE

My call up papers arrived on 21st September 1939. England had managed on its own for the first 18 warring days! However unlike as in later thrilling adventures, folk were to cry "the Navy's here", as though that meant some miraculous panacea or salvation. No one cried out to announce my arrival on the scene, which happened to be the roadway of the River Thames Embankment, London.

The only 'crying out' was done by a man in naval uniform wearing an unusual cap badge, later to be recognised as that of the "Master at Arms". This was the Navy's equivalent to a ship's Chief of Police. He bellowed at the hundred or so, bedraggled gathering of pimply faced youths, dressed in a wild assortment of suits, cut in various styles and cloths, all milling about aimlessly...

"GET FELL IN!" This order put an end to the ebbing and flowing of mob movement around the steps, which led to the gangway of *HMS PRESIDENT,* which served as the Flag Ship and HQ of the Royal Naval Volunteer Reserve otherwise known as RNVR - 'the Wavy Navy'. After a great deal of pushing and shoving, this 'bedragglement' was now a 'body of men', standing approximately in ranks of five deep alongside the kerb. I had got 'fell in' for the very first time in my young life! ... and awaited. I waited to see what happened next!

"SHUN!" bellowed the navy cap of strange design. Whereupon, one hundred pairs of (non jean) wrinkled trousers attempted to come together in vertical unison, somewhat ineffectively, be it confessed. The posture of these men was even more pathetic than the awful timing of this unsymmetrical, unsynchronised movement. Their appearance was not helped by the cardboard gas mask box strung diagonally across shoulders; some left: some right and although every box was government issue, it was surprising how every box jutted out or slid, on the hips, rump, waist or cradled on the thigh of its wearer, depending on how he was 'dressed' and the length of cord he choose in so doing. Never was there a mottlier crew, whatever that phrase means!

As we stood at what we believed was 'attention' the gloved hand on the outstretched arm of a 'Petty Officer' seemed to be flaying like a French policeman's between the rows. This practice seemed to be a favourite with Navy P.O.'s. It consisted of carving off sections or heaps of men/manpower into squads. They would be told to "Turn right - Double", on receipt of this instruction the whole group broke into a troupe of trotting zombies and continued trotting until they disappeared off the face of the earth.

This method of selection was the one which determined to which depot/naval establishment we were to be sent. It was learned afterwards that one brave body of 75 men were sent to HMS 'ROYAL ARTHUR' the new and excitingly reregistered name bestowed by the board of Admiralty on the Skegness Holiday Camp, loaned by Mr Billy Butlin for the duration of hostilities. Those trained here were known for ever after as "Skeggy Boys". Regardless of how far any naval depot or training academy was from the sea, they were all graced by the prefix HMS. Once entering any such establishment you had 'come aboard'. Going outside its walls was 'going ashore.' Land based, as most were, they were referred to as "Stone Frigates."

The rest of us were marched to Waterloo Station, passing several somnolent sphinxes sculptured in bronze, marble and granite, stretched out around the base of Cleopatra's needle. I swear that these layabouts we passed (not normally disturbed by the appalling sights seen everyday in London), did raise their eye-lids as this messy assortment of English youth passed by, on their way to war.

HMS Victory - A larger than life Stone Frigate

Arrival at *HMS Victory* - one of the three largest UK Naval Bases and my 'home base' was note-worthy only because of its novelty to us civilian bred gentlemen of very varied backgrounds, which seemed to drive some future instructors into paranoid spasms of incomprehension. When you answered their question "What were you in civilian life?" their response, was extraordinary. "You were what!?!" queried an empty head wearing a shiny peaked cap pulled well down over its forehead, along the rim of which travelled two eyes as though on a furtive silent curtain runner.

As we marched through the streets of Portsmouth, or Pompey which was 'navalesque' language and our future name for it, no bands played. No pretty girls strewed flowers in our path. In fact no one took the slightest notice at all, of the 25 new recruits now swinging beneath the Victorian concrete archway entrance to the barracks. Our appearance more resembled a batch of ill suited desperadoes on their way to overseas deportation on Devil's Island. This was *HMS Victory* which we had just 'come aboard.' Little did we know that from that moment on we had lost our individuality, identity and dignity. It was a case of "abandon hope all ye who enter here!"

We were inspected with some curiosity by the 'officer of the watch', which has little to do with chronology, and placed in the care of a three badge stripy rating, of some obvious naval experience an expert in artful dodging. He looked like he had just been featured in a remake of the ancient mariner. He led us away to commence the "joining routine." This routine is necessary to identify you as a fully joined up member of the ship's company having now come aboard. You must become vitalled. The main perks of this is, that you become entitled to draw a ration of grog every day at 11 a.m. when an announcement is made through the tannoy public address system, consisting of two words "Up Spirits." It also provides for issuing of every item of naval uniform according to your rating or rank, free of charge.

Our ancient mariner however was something else. His whole life having been spent confined to naval establishments, had severely restricted his vocabulary to a few basic noises and understandable phrases plus some universal sign language.

3

INITIAL TRAINING

Victory Barracks, Portsmouth. 1939
"Hookie Bruce"

Douglas on leave, 1939

At the tender age of 18 you are still adaptable, given the right sort of encouragement, understanding and help. Young persons can develop their natural abilities and with confidence, can go far. Everywhere except in the Royal Navy.

The accumulated wisdom of the senior service has been written up, set down, recorded, revised, re-recorded, amended, altered and, over many centuries, finally honed to the point where eventually, every variation of conduct and behaviour in every and any set of circumstances is covered, anticipated and catered for by onerous regulations. "KING'S RULES AND REGULATIONS" (With the backing of the death sentence if necessary!) This is no idle threat. Ultimately it can be enforced under existing English law. Fortunately it is or has been seldom implemented. The firing squad has not been called recently.

Thus there are rules, regulations, and routines almost like 'Holy Writ', in stone tablets and as inflexible as the law of the Meads and Persians. If you are wise, your best course of action is, therefore, to adapt to your new surroundings; to adopt the "when in Rome" attitude: stop reasoning, forget logic, forego common sense, do not question or argue, cease to kick against the pricks and especially those who happen to be running the local operations in which you are now involved! Instead, do what everyone else is doing, think only of your day of release. This is a little difficult to accomplish on the second day of your service for King and Country, but your mental attitude is all important because, as time passes, the lunacy gets worse!

But it is not all bad (in truth it never is: it is always your present state of mind). Indeed you are now just a number, one of many thousand look-alikes. You are now, to the outside world just another sailor; you can drop your guard. If you have lost your identity already why try to justify or maintain your personal reputation or self respect? You are a matelot and all the world knows what they are! So enjoy it.

Being a great believer in "life is what you make it" the writer set course for demob day by grasping the opportunities of each day, plundering the present possibilities, without much concern about tomorrow or any of the other days thereafter, no-one knew for sure if there were going to be any! War breeds its own morality – live for today, for tomorrow... you may not be alive to enjoy it! Hence looking back, although new found circumstances were not of one's choosing, they could be enhanced if one chose so to do, regardless of the volumes of King's regulations. A sense of humour is a great requisite.

Before being bungled off to sea we were given embarkation leave, the chance to show off ourselves to our nearest and dearest - in uniform for the first time! Whatever my family called me, to my girlfriend I was "Plonkie"! Can you imagine any more unlikely title for this fully trained decoding machine, dressed in his sailor suit, straining to join his shipmates and cover himself with imperishable glory! So long as she remained faithful to me, I did not care. I was deeply in love.

On leave (1939)

It was on one leave-taking morning, 14th November 1939, whilst in the city of London with my father that the news broke. Scapa's defences had been penetrated. A German U-boat had managed to sink the battleship *HMS ROYAL OAK* with a dreadful loss of life. Newly appointed "First Lord of the Admiralty", Mr Winston Churchill, had hurried north to restore the fleet's safe haven to its required level of security, but the shock waves swept the nation. This was a stark reminder that we really were at war.

WHAT DID YOU DO IN THE WAR, GRANDAD?

4

HMS Victory

Stone Frigate based at PORTSMOUTH

Reverting to our joining routine, hosted by our 'ancient Mariner'. This took up the best part of our first day. Accompanied by this worthy matelot, we progressed from the medical block to 'Administration'. From dental surgery' to the fitting out section, where we were sized up by the trained, yet unseeing eyes of' Wrens' (lady sailors of the Women's Royal Naval Service.) They threw bundles of blue serge at us. They were about as attractive as Dracula's daughters. If 'eyes are the windows of the soul...' even if the wearing of black stockings excited no increase of pulse rate, the fact was, the sight of these poor female eunuchs, would be more likely to lead a healthy male, to premature impotency.

If our eyes were being indoctrinated to strange, unaccustomed sights, our ears were also under bombardment. Twenty four hours ago we had left the bosom of our respective families, who to a greater or lesser extent, used words of the English language to communicate with one another to good effect.

As already mentioned our ancient Mariner was something else! His lack of lexicon dexterity was more than amply supplemented by words which polite persons would classify as "blue", vulgar or even profane. His language was unconventional and completely unacceptable in normal society. Even after six years war service, the writer cannot recall ever subsequently encountering a fouler mouthed individual, who was richer in outrageous expletives, and who persistently broke down words, of three or more syllables, inserting into the gaps thus created, a fruity full or part swear word. Even the most innocent object was cussed and cursed with an apocalyptical venom, approaching nihilistic proportions.

Why dwell on such a reminiscence? Only because one in retrospective bewilderment wonders, if either the passage of time has enriched the memory, of this poor illiterate man, to the point of exaggeration, on being so newly introduced to service life, or alternately to give him the much competed for title of "The World's Foulest Mouthed Abomination". Shakespeare would have learned a great deal!

Before leaving the audio aspect of our first day in the Royal Navy or "The Andrew" as it is called by the lower deck ratings (i.e. any lower rated serving member than a commissioned officer), the constant use of the public address system (tannoy) or 'blower' cannot be ignored. Bells were struck with varying significance, whistles or 'pipes' were blown, not to mention the occasional blasts from bugles! All these sounds were intended to notify us of some important feature of the day's activity or routine, that needed additional emphasis The constant repartee was insistent, sustained and utterly sapping. It destroyed conversation, transcended all thought and even wrought inaction. You moved like programmed 'zombies'. Next day and for all the next several days we were to be trained. Each man turned from being a useless piece of civilian flotsam into a clear headed master of whatever subject we had previously expressed a preference in, with quick reactions.

It is true that the choice of subjects offered by the Navy is not very wide. Not much room for 'gardening' for example. However my subject had been predetermined; I wanted to be in 'signals'. A signalman or in naval terms a "Bunting Tosser." A member of the communications visual branch. The appeal was that this was the only branch which offered the participant an opportunity of learning what was 'going on'. All messages of any importance were of course coded, but plain language was used to a great extent and thus understood, not by all, but by most.

The language used by Chief Yeoman and Yeomen of Signals was mostly only too plain. They seemed to have a mysterious knowledge concerning your immediate and past heredity. Usually this knowledge inferred that you lacked a parental pedigree. The Communication Branch consisted of two quite separate divisions

1) Wireless telegraphy

2) Visual Signals.

Both required acquiring total understanding and knowledge of the Morse code either by ear or eye.

The branch was known as the "Intelligence branch", the description being applied to the pure context of communication and not to the sagacity of the individual, although most of us knew our alphabet and some of us could actually read! The lessons for those training to become wireless telegraphists, meant sitting for hour after hour locked away from all human distraction, wearing earphones, listening unceasingly to Morse characters being transmitted at ever increasing speeds. Day after day the same performance. Classes of would-be telegraphists would sit with pen and paper known as a signal pad, in front of a tapping key to send and/or receive messages, entirely made up of five numerical blocks. Page after page, until you became proficiently perfect, absolutely accurate 'at the rate of knots'. Can you imagine anything more mind blowing as an activity? Thank goodness I decided to train for visual signals i.e. flags, flashing lights, lights, boys beacons and above all fresh air.

In stark contrast to our telegraphic brothers, who were seen aboard ship only when they emerged from their turn or 'duty-watch' from some dingy, airless, drab, overcrowded and cramped compartment stuffed well below the waterline, protected by the armour plating to the joys of the 'bunting tossers', who faced the outside real world of screaming sea-gulls and the best or worst of mother nature's weather moods! Our training was also done in the open air. We spent our time reading semaphore flags (Morse flags were a non-starter) or the flashing light of Morse code spelling out verbal plain English language words which had their own meaning and usually made some sort of sense when read back. On other occasions the series being transmitted was a selection of jumbled up letters and numbers which were each to be instantly recognised and recorded. We would stand in couples, one facing the lamp source, the other with his back to the light, recording whatever was shouted out. This standard practice was conducted hour after hour, day after day, week after week. Practice makes perfect.

However this stage in this signalman's life was very much in the future. I was employed and enrolled in the initial course as a 'de-coder' - the very lowest form of naval life described for record purposes as Ordinary Signalman Coder - candidate Arthur D. Bruce. My glorious military title hardly qualified me to walk under a snake wearing a top hat – even if I removed the top hat! A sub-zero rating. What a job! You were trained to use decoding devices but only in part. You would never be allowed to read the message which you had helped to unravel. That final satisfaction was left to a superior mind. Someone higher up the intelligence ladder.

On joining HIS ROYAL BRITTANIC NAVY you have to learn many things very quickly, one of which is proving the adage "that there is plenty for all, if you are quick enough!" Having spent the first day (22nd September 1939) of my non-illustrious career at VICTORY BARRACKS, PORTSMOUH by going through "the joining routine", where, if you react to having a fork stuck into you they pronounce that you are still warm and therefore alive enough to be allowed "in" and spent some of a small allowance they provided for clothing i.e. a naval uniform and top wear etc. you soon learn the lesson of looking after what is "yours."

During my first night ever sleeping in a hammock, I had my brand new lovely "going ashore" heavy navy blue No. 1 overcoat... stolen! The thief cut the hanging tag and dropped it noiselessly into his waiting arms as quietly as the heavenly dew drops to earth. One silent slice of a sharp razor... it fell without disturbing the lightest of sleepers. I had learnt my first lesson in self-preservation. It reminded me of a 'tall tale' told by my own father. He recounted the following story: It was of a Jewish dad who told his only son to stand on the kitchen table and to jump down into his waiting arms. After the child jumped in obedience and gone crashing down, falling on his face, blacking both his eyes and bleeding from his now toothless mouth - he heard his father say "My boy, that's your first lesson in life... never trust anybody".

If I hated figures at school, my hatred was intensified to white heated anger because my young useful life was now doomed to the mindless treadmill of a de-coder. My first duty in His Majesty's Service and to the total war effort had been the training I had just received over the last two or three weeks to turn me into someone whose job it was to undo naval codes from numbers into 'plain numbers'... not plain language but more numbers. We were now considered competent enough to go on active service! We de-coders never were allowed to know or understand the messages sent in code. We were just part of the process, the crushingly incomprehensibly boring process, of 'undoing' the code, to enable an officer, (preferably one who could read and write), to refer to the code books for the meaning of these blocks of five numbers each of which, would become a recognisable real life living "word".

A coder's life aboard any naval ship was four hours off duty roughly every four hours, shut away near the wireless room. The signal pad was ruled in such a way to aid you to carry out your instructions to do this. Having done this you handed your pad, now a mass of blocks of numbers, to the officer of the watch. Believe me it was tedious, boring to the point of suicide! It was a job at which you laboured ceaselessly without the slightest trace of "job satisfaction". Thus with my companions drawn from other branches (signals visual, telegraphists, engineers, stokers, seamen and writers etc) we formed the recruitment requirement for the commissioning of *HMS Canton* which was currently occupying the berth made famous by its previous occupant, the 534 or better known as the original RMS *"Queen Mary"*. Hence our draft chit meant entraining at Portsmouth for this Clydeside destination.

One of my decoding colleagues is worthy of special mention. His real name escapes my memory, but his nick name was the "Professor". Everyone for some reason had to have a 'nick name' in His Majesty's employment. Like myself, 'The Prof' was scooped off the Thames embankment and also like me tried hard to keep his composure when the cultural shock and change of lifestyle hit his day by day realisation. I felt for this man with something approaching awe! He had elected to serve in the intelligent branch with some justification. He had, after all, obtained a university degree. He had 'an ology!' Whilst he was no intellectual, compared with his present superiors in their peaked caps, he was a genius, no Socrates or Plato, yet here he was. Another of his outstanding talents was his ability to wring a tune out of a genuine squeeze-box (the old hexagonal shape sort of concertina). Finally, he was heavily bearded. It reached from ear to ear and covered his chin and cheeks with a thick black fuzzy mat. Two sparklingly bright eyes pierced through all this, to complete almost photographically the portrait so prominently displayed on the advertisement hoardings and on every packet of that famous brand of John Players cigarettes.

Sleeping was described as "crashing the bonce". This non-activity usually happened each day following the dispensation of the daily rum ration. Servants of the flag could and would be found lying prone, completely comatose on any flat surface large enough to carry them.

At this stage of the narrative, it seems appropriate to outline the part that RUM played in the daily saga of naval service life in the navy of 1940. The practice of issuing rum has now ceased but only after a history dating back to Nelson's days. The practice was originally introduced for medicinal reasons. There was a marked absence of medics, doctors, nurses or anyone with an ounce of medical practice aboard any of Nelsons' men o'war ships. You can imagine the horrors of naval engagements... crashing masts falling with sails on fire falling upon the hapless heads of the gun-crews on the open decks. Splinters of wood, of blown apart oak beams and snipers' bullets from unreliable shot guns whistling through clouds of choking smoke. No wonder Nelson lost an eye! It was the practice of drugging the "fallen" comrades by the administering of intoxicants to relieve the excruciating pain for those seriously wounded. Rum was the only way out. They died with a smile on their faces! Thus, right up to this time (WW2) rum was important to lower deck ratings of His Majesty's Royal Britannic Navy. Its uses were manifold. It became currency. You could 'buy' things with it... a cosy balaclava, or a pair of weatherproof gloves. You could celebrate a birthday, an anniversary, wedding date, or even ease the pain of mourning at a funeral. It was a panacea for all sorts of ills. It could steady the nerves in action if used wisely and it could also kill when abused.

Without doubt it has always been my belief that I would not have been able to survive the terrible weather conditions of those Russian convoys, had I not been able to bring back to life those 'frozen' extremities of my legs arms etc, after four frightening hours of duty watch, on the upper bridge of those destroyers. For a fortnight, I seldom was able to keep down any food I attempted to eat. Lack of any nourishment, lack of a good night's sleep and the sheer effort of living out each ghastly day, in sub-zero temperatures, days without proper daylight except between 11am and 2pm, wallowing in seas of overwhelmingly frightening ferocity... just the normal stress of staying alive, surviving for another day. It was absolutely crucifying.

I am not a drinker, but I cannot claim to be a TT either. Rum saved this writer's life. To avoid the obvious danger of serving alcohol to the watch on deck, which undoubtedly altered the course of history (on more than one occasion) the "tot" of those on duty, would be carefully secured by watchful mates below decks. Hence the grog call "Up Spirits" sounded at 11am daily until the change of the watch at 12.30pm was faithfully observed, so that the realm was never jeopardised by the incautious dispensation of intoxicants. In passing, the all too rare occasions of a visit by royalty, was usually celebrated by the most welcome command ever issued (and only by the reigning monarch) of "Splice the mainbrace"... or serve a double portion of the golden Jamaican elixir of Navy life!

5

FIRST TIME TO SEE THE SEA

October 1939 Aboard the HMS CANTON (Armed Merchant Cruiser)

HMS Canton – P&O Cruiser, converted to armed merchant cruiser used to patrol areas of sea.

HMS Canton was about a year old. War had broken out whilst she was at Hong Kong on her maiden voyage. This ship was the newest addition to the fleet built by P&O, their latest luxury cruising liner. Tonnage about 16,000 catered for first and second class passengers only. Speed approximatley max 20 knots, oil fired, sleek, well ventilated and exceedingly comfortable - in the tropics, (although she did not have modern central heating.) She was to serve as an armed (eight, 6" guns) merchant cruiser off Iceland! The gap left by the recent sinking of *HMS Rawalpindi* on the Northern Patrol had to be plugged.

The stretch of inhospitable ocean which stretches between the north of Scotland and Iceland was to become familiar to the writer during the next four years of conflict. The stationing of ships ploughing backwards and forwards along set lines of patrol was aimed at providing a screen through which vessels should not pass without challenge, or at least Admiralty knowledge. (*HMS Rawalpindi* another Armed Merchantman, crewed by South African Royal Naval volunteers, very bravely challenged a German pocket battleship, who answered her challenge, by sinking her!) Replacing her was like putting another pair of false teeth (*HMS Canton*) in place of a pair that had been unfairly and very brutally knocked out.

It was, and probably still is, an area of glassy-greeny-grey water. Some places on this earth are not improved, even when the sun shines upon them. Rotherham is one, the Northern Patrol is another. Members already serving in the Merchant Navy were retained. Absorbed by the navy they were termed as "124" ratings and they fell under the authority of senior service personnel. They were the only ones who really knew what they were doing! They could *drive* the thing! Their scorn for the quality of Royal Navy seamanship was evident. It was unkindly repeated that they held the view that many an R.N. skipper could not turn his ship around, whilst land remained in sight! It was true that on a large number of recently commissioned sea going vessels, new members of the seagoing fraternity, were doing a considerable amount of damage to the British coastline, whilst endeavouring to get their charges *out of the garage*. However T124 ratings were to be of the small experienced number of *Canton's* ship's company. They had at least driven her to China and back without damaging her paint work.

The morning dawned bright and clear for the arrival of a requisitioned trainload of navy personnel destined to take her out to sea. The Scottish weather was kind and allowed a mountain of kit bags to be piled high on the quayside, without getting drenched, with what Scots call Scotch mist and everyone else calls rain! Baggage reclaim, even to this day, is an art in itself. I had learned another lesson: Make yours *very distinctive*. This is still a good tip for air travellers today. I had achieved this by painting the underside end of my kit bag (the end furthest away from the tying cord) red and white, with black block letters indicating it belonged to Anno Domini Bruce. Thus I was quickly able to settle in my berth several decks below water level on *Canton's* "E" deck. As it took about twenty minutes, at a hard rush, to "action" and work stations in the wireless office on "B" deck, we were offered the unparalleled luxury, of a four berthed cabin on the life-boat deck, much, much nearer our place of duty. This cabin equipped with its own wash hand basin, wall cupboard, wooden louvered shutter and squareport (window) of generous dimensions. It was absolutely super, it would have been costly, even for a first class passenger. But our work in the decoding office next to the wireless office was 'critical' and thus needed to be strategically placed to fulfil it. There were no TV or "teasmaid" contraptions in those days, but we did enjoy plenty of open deck fresh air, which whistled along the open "Boat deck". Finally and in addition, we had overhead bedside lighting, controllable ship's radio volume control, plus beds rather than hammocks in which to sleep!

Such RN shipboard sleeping accommodation was never again to be experienced! The whole interior of this vessel was beautifully fitted out. Our second class dining room still had potted plants although these disappeared mysteriously one by one very quickly! The unauthorised removal of naval items was unfortunately, common practice. Useful household objects were "liberated" and smuggled "down the line" to unknown landward destinations. Such items were referred to as "rabbits" and so those so engaged were advised by bystanders to "tuck their ears in". The restaurant walls were teak panelled and still looked elegant, even though the ship was being prepared for sea, the full length wall mirrors had been removed as a safeguard against flying splinters of shattering glass caused by gun fire. We luxuriated in padded leather fully upholstered carver chairs, grouped around protected eating surfaces, each with its hinged drop down table edge, which could be raised to prevent plates etc slipping off under stormy weather conditions.

The *Canton* was a lovely ship when she first fell into the hands of the Royal Navy. In anticipation of the approaching war, the Admiralty had decreed that her decks, when being built should be suitably strengthened to take six inch guns (of which she had six, plus four 4" and an aircraft catapult launcher). I never it saw used, possibly because we had no planes to launch! Soon with almost indecent haste, we slipped our berth and proceeded away from John Brown's yard, to meander down the Clyde, passing Dumbarton Rock, the tail of the bank, Greenock, through the Cloch lighthouse, boom defence across to Dunoon, thence onward to pass Rothesay, the Cumbraes, towards Arran, Aisla Craig and the open sea. Stand by, Hitler... here we come!

ACTIVE SERVICE

Before taking up our station and whilst still en route to it, a rushed period of "working up" was needed. This was intended to familiarise the ship's company with her capabilities, geography and action stations, fire drill, gunnery, fire fighting and any emergency routines. During one of these gunnery practises one of the port forward guns which all had appropriate location numbers i.e. "P" for port 1, 2, 3, 4, matched by Starboard 1, 2, 3, 7, 4, blasted off their round much bellowing of yellow cordite and noise, which had the effect of inflicting damage to the forward bulkhead door, which had not been properly secured. Thus this door was somehow lifted off its very substantial hinges and flew up and over the ship's side! Several tons of armour plated metal, it made a very sensational flying missile and splash. Whilst aboard *Canton*, I never again heard another gun fired in fun or anger.

November of 1939 was the beginning of a cruel winter. We had an atrocious spell of about six weeks, shunting backwards and forwards along an allotted patrol line, working in three watches round the clock. Time passed without any sightings whatsoever and thankfully therefore no incidents. Never was I at any time of my naval career in the mood for heroics. They were strictly for others of sterner stuff or breeding... I was a natural born, well adjusted grade "A" coward! I was quite happy to leave the clever stuff to Hollywood's Mr. Eroll Flynn (film star). However, our problems were about to overtake us.

With the normal and most accurate navigational aids, we were struggling (radar had been invented but it was not as yet fitted into *Canton's* defences). Even in those days we had not had the comfort of confirming our charted position, by taking any usual compass and visual fix on sun or stars, for several days. Visibility was very poor, limited and daylight exceedingly short. We were navigating by dead reckoning. Asking for a radio fix was not allowed as 'radio silence' was absolute. Clouds and general murk prevented the use of old aged navigational implements. We were relying on automatic pilot "George". Having served our appointed span of patrol (four weeks) we set course for home.

I remember the monotony of those watches well; alone in the decoding office/cabin, busy doing half a job! A small hatch divided us from the ship's wireless office. I took an instant dislike to the T124 radio officer, who delighted to burst the hatch door almost off its hinges, as he thrust signal after signal, through for our attention. Never a word! Just this bloated face and puffy fingers stuffing the papers through, as though into an oven. He obviously hated us "wavy navy" lads. We reciprocated his loathing. It was whilst on duty on the evening of 7th January 1940 about 2320 (11.20pm) that I felt a very unusual motion hit the ship. After some weeks or more you attune to the creaks, moans, groans and normal movement in any ship at sea, but this was different and most unlike any experienced so far. It went on for several minutes, seemed to steady, then to recommence as though the ship was now going astern. We had... HIT THE ROCKS!!! We had run into the southernmost end of the Isle of Barra, on the outer Hebrides - and it hadn't shifted! Not bad for my first attempt to "go to sea"!

6

SHIPWRECK

The bow of the *Canton* had lifted and run over some rocks in an underwater reef and the ship had come to rest. As we 'reversed' a great gash was ripped in the forward part of the ship's hull, the length of the two forward holds. Later someone described this as "a banana skin being peeled back". Orders were issued to "abandon ship". It was a nasty night for this caper. Leaving the privacy and warmth of my coding office, I stepped out onto the boat deck. Squalls of rain swept across the well scrubbed deck, driven-by wild gusts of unfriendly gale force winds. Nature can terrify one. We assembled at our life boat, were "accounted for" and awaited the next command. It didn't come for some time. The ship by now was clear of the reef and slanting forward - "down by the head" to be nautical. Fortunately the bulkheads were holding the pressure of the water, even though both forward holds were completely flooded. The order came eventually to repair to "action stations" but remain on "grade-one state of readiness".

What a relief! To creep back bedraggled, but thankful to be in the shelter of the coding office. Without fully appreciating the dire circumstances in which the *Canton* found herself, here was warmth, four walls and familiar objects which seemed safer than the hell that was howling outside. Folk on the *Titanic* must have felt the same way. This isn't happening, but it was. Through the wall, shadowy figures in wet watch-coats came and went. Signals were obviously being sent. And so the long, long night passed. No-one was allowed to "go below". Dawn broke, a grey murky affair with somewhat moderated winds. Rumour had it that "young members" of the ship's company were to be "transferred" - but to what? And to where? No land visible and certainly as yet no ship was in sight, friend or foe. The rumour had absolutely no foundation. It was pure fantasy!

We were then released from watch - I had been on duty since 8.00pm, and it was now 8.00am. We reported for breakfast in the second class tourist restaurant, our communication mess, without being asked twice! Nothing to eat was available other than the previous night's baking of bread - but this was delicious. It had been over cooked and was still in the ovens until they were closed down much later than intended. Normally, navy food was perfect when purchased, but the way it was cooked was little short of criminal. However, this black crusted, new bread was a feast for kings and "queens" (we had a few of the latter aboard).

A short time after mid-day, a sight greeted our eyes that I shall never forget. *HMS Canton* had come backwards off the reef, stern first for navy personnel - gone down by the head, but survived by making very slow progress ahead. I don't remember just how many knots. She was well built, watertight bulkheads and doors were "holding fast" even though both hold were full with Atlantic Ocean sea water. We were heading south, around the notoriously wild Outer Hebrides - destination either Belfast or the Clyde - some hundreds of miles away. We were alone, a sitting duck. One well-placed depth charge or Christmas cracker would have blown our bulkheads. Suddenly, and it seemed from all parts of the compass, sleek grey silhouettes dashed, each with a "bone in its teeth" converged upon us. These were destroyers of the 8111 Home Fleet Flotilla! At least we had company, a trouble shared is a trouble halved. Signals were exchanged and they formed an escort screen around us on all sides. We plopped, waddled and wallowed along at seemingly no knots at all. Even jelly fishes thumbed their noses at us as they swam past.

Our destination was said to be the Clyde - and so it was. With shame we lumbered round the Mull of Kintyre, ploughed past the Holy Isle, the Cumbrae light, past Toward Point and through the boom at the Clough lighthouse. To take refuge at the far sandy end of the Holy Loch close by Sandbank - bow first - beached on the soft volcanic grey soil which they called sand. We were grounded deliberately to prevent further risk to the bulkheads - at the very far end of the Holy Loch. Thus ended the ignominy, our swashbuckling sally to sea.

But once over the excitement and gratitude of being saved - we found there were other things to do. An account had to be given by those responsible for the near loss of the ship - a court martial was organised. More pleasantly - leave to the ship's company. One half at a time could be allowed, whilst repairs were effected. It meant two lots of 14 days each, spread over the total repair time. This was fabulous.

My folks did not expect to see me again until "Britannia ruled the waves" - but here I was. A fully bloodied survivor, home again - and my name wasn't "Bill Bailey". November 1939, and leave after only a few weeks service!

Even when on shipboard duty between leaves, life aboard was beginning to become enjoyable.

Repair leave at Holy Loch

Romance in the navy in those far off days was strictly associated with the nearness of land! Beached high and dry on firm sand, surrounded by scenic beauty of unsurpassed grandeur, Scotland is the poor man's Switzerland. The glens, the lochs, the waterfalls were beautiful. Along the shore road which hugs the lochside, people of wealth, whether honestly accumulated or not, had their homesteads. Green lawns with flag poles and some with brass canons facing seaward. Retired seafarers no doubt luxuriating away their last days - smoking shag, sipping stags breath and cackling cogitative, conjections to their club cronies. They were in for a shock!

It was obvious that if *Canton's* bows were to be repaired it was necessary to get her up river and into dry dock. Her draft was 26 feet normally - but now the forward part was greatly in excess of that. So the brilliant proposal was to lift her 'head' by pumping air into the holds having first made sure that the forward compartments could take the pressure of sealing the deck plates and the holds to make them absolutely watertight. Easier said than done. Nevertheless work had begun to do this. First all the rotten and rotting food floating about in the flooded holds had to be 'got rid'. You cannot just throw that volume overboard in confined waters. Orderly method was called for. We would use the ship's lifeboats as 'ullage skips' they were mobile so once filled could be moved. So they were to be towed to the shore at high tide and emptied into large holes in the sand buried out of sight, sound and smell! This work went on for several days. This seemed to be a highly successful method in the circumstances. Burial almost 'at sea.'

But the unexpected happened. To quote the Scottish Bard "the best laid plans of mice and men oft' go 'agley'. Four lifeboats, loaded to the gunnels, were alongside as darkness fell. They were full of the holds garbage, in readiness for early morning disposal. However they broke loose in a strong wind, and gently drifted ashore, tipped and spread their content liberally on the fair of Sandbank shoreline. Every seagull in the U.K. got the message! By mid-forenoon a grey-whitish cloud of squawking, mist formed overhead as thousands of every sort of gull, massed, swirled, squabbled, screamed, in a chaos of flying aerobatics. By nightfall the damage had been done!

Daylight dawned. The scene was horrific. The Holy Loch was one holy mess! It was decorated, it dripped, was festooned, with cascades of half decomposed, meat, stinking fish and unfrozen rotten vegetables of wide variety. Flag poles were dressed with it, lawns were strewn with it, and brass canons were garlanded with it. It was quite a 'to do' to put it mildly! Weeks were subsequently spent by ship working parties clearing up the debris from every place and as well as some very unlikely places! (No one was heard to shout with enthusiasm "The Navy's here!" Rather more likely the saying about "stinking in the nostrils of honest men".)

It was customary each Sunday for a church party to be sent ashore to the local parish church. This was about a mile from the landing jetty. Thus rows of sailors dressed in their "Number Ones", their very best public formal uniforms, would be paraded, inspected and disembarked into one or two of the ship's lifeboats and "row for the shore lads". It was noticeable that the popularity of church attendance was gaining ground, a curious phenomenon, considering most navy personnel, were normally only familiar with places of spiritual dispensing which had "push" in brass lettering on both doors! Curiosity aroused, I decided to join the 'Sabbath going ashore' worshippers. It was not long before a race developed to reach the jetty. Muscles strained and expletives flew, as the levers were 'yanked' back and forwards with tremendous energy as the two heavy steel lifeboat hulls were propelled through the tranquil waters of the Holy Loch at the rate of knots. After getting 'fell-in' on the jetty, the church party sped off at a brisk marching pace; boots clicked in unison, as we swung along the shore road - bell bottoms legs swinging in answer to the peel of the church bell. (This was a church where one bell was considered enough! Everything was rationed in these days).

The mystery of the excursion was soon dispelled. On the shouted order from the senior rating of this squad, a purple nosed three-badged, beery-looking Able-bodied seaman - the party smartly "left wheeled" behind a local wayside pub, nestling on the lochside. The front doors apparently shut, bolted and barred. Remember this was Scotland... and this was the Sabbath... but the rear bar entrance opened as by magic at the chance of early morning trade. Very swift 'bevies' of booze rapidly disappeared down thirty, very thirsty throats, almost without touching the sides. Thus encouraged, the subsequent hymn singing benefited greatly. 'Those who perished on the seas' would at least die with a smile on their faces! Our convoy back to the ship would also be somewhat erratic, thus showing we believed in zigzagging, to fool any lurking U-boats.

The DAY OF COURT MARTIAL dawned. All involved with damaging the ship were being called to account. Senior and some junior personnel were required to attend in full No.1 Uniform. Thus officers in full regalia, shoulder epaulets, ceremonial swords, golden carrots etc. The venue was the offices of Commander in Chief Clyde, situated on the pier head, at Gourock overlooking the important and packed "Tail of the Bank" moorage area. This anchorage is the last really deep water before the river Clyde narrows down to a permanently dredged channel, extending up river, past Port Glasgow, Dumbarton Rock, Erskine and the numerous shipbuilding yards on route to central Glasgow. This was the home of Clydebuilt boats.

It was about three nautical miles from our position, beached on the soft sand of Sandbank Bay in the Holy Loch. It was ideal for the assembly of ships forming up for convoy duties, to Russia and, of course, to America and the rest of the world. It was thus full of a polyglot of vessels and crews of every description, and every nation. At night in the strictest of 'Blackouts' the operation of getting this mob, now very full of local brew and sundry other refreshments was chaotic. Streets full of reeling arguing, shouting, brawling matelots, reluctantly bore down shipward towards Custom House quay, where awaited scores of hired Drifters, side by side, up to five deep, moored in batches, alongside the quays. Each Drifter was destined for one ship only, somewhere out there in the blackness. The skipper repeatedly shouting out his Drifter's ship destination to which crew members were required to join.

The tumult was unbelievable. Some were so drunk that they fell between quay and drifter, and in the darkness were posted "as absent without leave" not only from their ship, but this world also. Several took a long walk off a short plank. I recall seeing a rating slip overboard, watching him bob up again still with his "tickler" (home-rolled cigarette) still clenched between his teeth and still wearing his hat! What is more remarkable that so many actually found their way home and boarded the right drifter.

That was the town, the nerve centre of our ship's motor launch was making for, on this dull morning, but in full daylight. I am told that the launch's engine developed a cough and began to 'sound a bit rough'. It appeared to be a bit noisier than usual as it bobbed across the three miles. It was however just about to complete its passage and had almost reached the shore when the bottom opened up and the engine fell through. The launch floundered immediately, dumping its highly dressed occupants, chest high, at low tide, in seaweedy, slushy water. Bedraggled but without further loss, they reported for sentencing. The *Greenock Telegraph* had some telling pictures for their publication that week. Our decks were strengthened and air pumped to 'Lift' our head. *HMS Canton* was finally towed up river and after some six to eight weeks, we were made ready for active service once again.

Onboard HMS Canton

7

NEAR MISS

After repair, *Canton* sailed for Portland. We witnessed helplessly the Dunkirk Evacuation before sailing towards Tenerife. One day as we were gently returning from the tropics and being off duty at about two o'clock in the afternoon I was having a relaxing swim in the very lovely ship's swimming pool. Suddenly, *"ACTION STATIONS"* blared out on the tannoy. *HMS Canton* was being attacked by a German U-boat. A torpedo was seen travelling at speed, approaching our starboard bow, clearly leaving a white trial in its wake. I arrived at my 'action station' on the flag deck dressed in a tin hat and swimming trunks!

No explosion! It passed within 3 feet in front, yet still underneath the ship's prow. A second later it would have hit us! A second torpedo was still a strong possibility. It did not happen however. We will never know why. We increased to full speed and swung away to port to reduce our broad outline. She was capable of a fairly good turn of 18/19 knots. What a near miss.

We made it back to Portsmouth without further incident. Armed Merchant Cruiser *HMS Canton* was missed by a whisker. We were "berthed" in Poole harbour, awaiting further orders. A few miles up the coast, Dunkirk was in full swing. We were a bit too large as a Passenger Cruise ship of 16,000 ton to be of any use in the shallow waters of Dunkirk. We stood by, in case of being needed and watched helplessly, as 'paddle steamers' brought shiploads of broken spirited, wounded, bewildered and broken members of our defeated army home. Why was *Canton* berthed in Portland? This is pure rumour but could it possibly have been to evacuate the Royal Family? They refused to go anywhere and stayed home whilst the invasion of Great Britain was being planned. Dunkirk was going on only a few miles away.

We spent our time exercising with *HMS Black Swan* (of later fame in the Far East escape down river.) A junker Nazi bomber flew a few feet over our funnel one forenoon. He could have dropped his lunch box down our funnel, he was so low. (When asked, my brother said, his nearest war-time miss, was from a flying doughnut thrown in a NAFFI canteen!) It was during this visit that I was transferred, at my request, from being a 'de-coder' to training to become a bona fide signalman on the visual side of the communication division. This meant becoming a "bunting tosser". Our job was to use all sort of equipment... semaphore hand flags, flashing lamps, hoisting large flags, to send visual signals. This was an active fresh air job, usually on the upper bridge whilst at sea. We were called the 'intelligent dept'... and some of us could actually read and write!

At this time German bombers were paying regular visits to soften up all south coast towns, in preparation for landing their invasion armies. Our training was frequently interrupted by air raids. We spent several hours down in trenches two feet below the barrack ground. I recall another near miss when one stick of five bombs straddled Victory's parade ground. Before the dust blotted out my eyes, I remember seeing the concrete wall in front of my bench seat bending out toward me, like a chest breathing in, filling itself, before restraining and returning to its proper state. We discovered after that raid that a large hole had been blown a few feet away.

8

A New Station

AT my own request I was transferred from de-coding work, and under-took the training to become a bona fide signalman, working on the visual side of the comunications division.

Training was back at *HMS Victory*, but it wasn't long before I 'caught a draft chit'. I was to be posted to *HMS Maidstone*, along with six other worthies of varying rank and rating, and all of us were put on a train at Portsmouth, destined to join our new ship at Rosyth on the Firth of Forth.

To our surprise, no-one there seemed to be expecting us - and no-one cared. What's more, no-one seemed to know where *HMS Maidstone* was. She certainly wasn't at Rosyth.

Rumour had it she had sailed for Gibraltar, a possibility which made our pulses beat fast at the prospect of sun, sand and sultry Spanish maidens frolicking in the surf. Sadly the reality was somewhat less exotic: *HMS Maidstone* was acting as a submarine depot ship, based at Scapa Flow in the Orkney Islands.

My first impression of Thurso - a name which still sends shivers down my spine - was formed lying on my back, spread flat along a seat in an ice:cold railway carriage as our marathon train journey from Portsmouth neared its end.

I watched a seagull trying to fly itself out of trouble in the face of a force ten thermal which threatened to blow the bird inside out. On opening the carriage door, a blast of the coldest wind shot up our bell bottoms - it was like arriving at the end of the world.

Never did I feel so far from civilisation. The only ferry from Scrabster, on which Scapa depended greatly, was suspended as gales lashed the coast. We spent three nights sleeping on the wooden block floor of the town hall, but we were soon to learn the meaning of the word 'discomfort' when we boarded the steamer *St Ninian,* the only passenger ferry between the top of Scotland and the Orkney Islands.

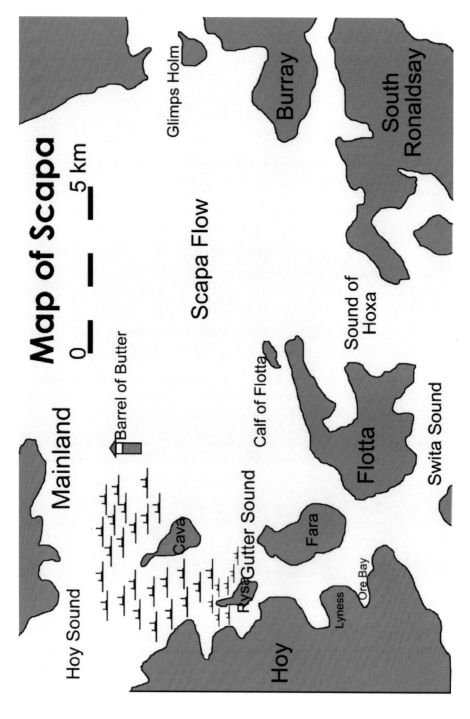

HMS Maidstone

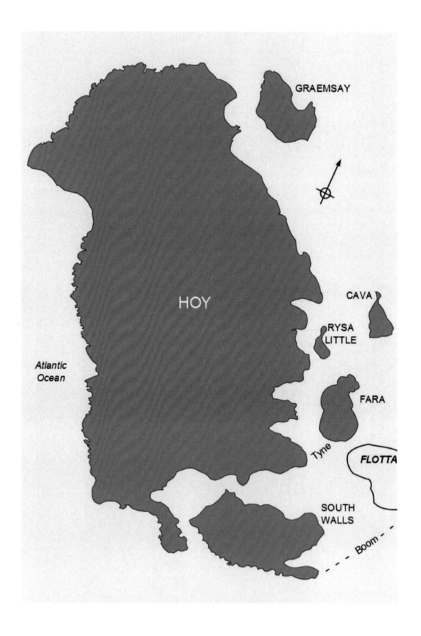

St Ninian was a ship of noble outline. She looked good sitting in the water, and she had the suspicion of a saucy rake to her funnel and masts, but her appearance belied the stark, basic shelter she afforded to the black huddles of humanity she transported regularly across the unfriendly and often ferocious currents of the Pentland Firth.

The entrances to the fleet anchorages at Scapa were, of course, mined; a circuitous route was necessary, and meant offering the ship side-on to the prevailing weather conditions. We huddled together like Antarctic penguins on the upper deck. Once safe, inside the boom, we looked in vain for other signs of life or comfort. Nothing! Grey ships, a gasometer and a cluster of Nissen huts, plus one rectangular building which served as the fleet canteen.

Large warships anchored under the lee of the islands of Hoxa and Flotta. Gutter Sound, between Flotta and the much larger island of Hoy, was crowded with destroyers, frigates, small ships and escort vessels. There was a line of about 18 buoys at which one, sometimes two, vessels would berth. About half way down this line were supply ships, a floating dry dock and *HMS Maidstone,* our destination.

Scapa, in those early days of the war, was a bleak, bleak place - cold, cheerless and totally populated by male naval personnel The total absence of female personnel resulted in the whole place looking scruffy, run down and uncared for, before then many men went unshaven, warmly but sloppily shod and clothed, and wearing home knitted balaclavas.

WRNS - Womens Royal Navy Service
The wren was the nickname given to them.

WRENS at Scapa brings to mind a story heard by a fly on the wall. No responsibility is taken for its authenticity. We go back to the days when Scapa was about to accept these lovely creatures and welcome them into an "all male" society. The Chief WREN was in conversation with the Orkney's boss man, Admiral in Charge Orkney & Shetland (ACOS). The Admiral expressed that many would find it difficult to retain their virginity.

The Chief Wren replied, tapping her temple, "Don't worry about my girls, they have it up here!"

The Admiral replied "I don't care where they have got it, my boys will find it!"

Before the Wren invasion it was almost impossible to arrange a 'date' with a female. The nearest members of the fair sex worked in the office of the

Chief Naval Command or Orkney and Shetland in Kirkwall, the capital of the islands. The passing of frequent telephone messages from the *Tyne* to this nerve-centre meant that we could talk to the imagined lovely creatures. Slowly we built up an enhanced identikit picture of each to match the silky, siren-smooth and sexy voices. No doubt the girls laid it on thick – after all they were safe from assault (except verbal) on the telephone. Banalities were exchanged for hours, especially during the night watches – when messages were almost non-existent, heart-to-heart confessions and fantasy flowed both ways during these exchanges.

Finally permission was granted for Wrens to visit the Lyness base but only on parties of three at a time. Safety in odd numbers. It was right across, or rather around, the three mile reach of the flow itself. The Kirkwall Ferry was an open drifter with no seating of any sort, apart from the gunwale. A blind date was arranged. Three of us and three of them. Six people in one go would meet for the first time and spend a couple of hours in each other's company. A watch mate of mine and an inoffensive and dull telegraphist made up our party. It was agreed to be ashore in time to meet the girls on the landing stage at Lyness, when the Kirkwall Drifter arrived. What happened after that, we would leave to chance and the imagination.

Thus three exceptionally smart sailors, all immaculately turned out in their number one uniforms, polished shoes, freshly washed and ironed blue sailor collars, complete with tiddly bow, stood hopefully and apprehensively at the very end of the jetty, scanning every arriving drifter. Finally one was sighted, not far off, and approaching with unusual silhouettes stationed in the bows. "Horses!" someone muttered! "Oh good grief! Look at them!" exclaimed my mate as we gazed transfixed by the sight of three of the plainest looking, unfeminine ladies of advanced years imaginable, at least in their 30s. But in these specimens, nature had provided a grossly unfair handout, when dishing out basic equipment. Uniforms do little for the form of the fair sex. "Dracula's daughter" grunted Sparks, "Let's make a bee line for the fleet canteen." Grabbing him between us, we pointed out that though we shared his feelings, we couldn't show such base conduct. We were trapped. The ferry tied up alongside halfway down the landward end of the jetty, cutting off our retreat to the shore. Besides there we were, three twits "dressed up like a dog's dinner" in sharp contrast to all those around us, we were their obvious "dates." Bananas would be a far more fitting description.

The gentlemanly action was taken. It couldn't be avoided. Introductions done and pairing off, with several yards regulation distance between each couple, we trod the well worn walk towards the Martello tower. All passionate fantasies had long since evaporated. No gun turrets swivelled to watch our progress. No telescopes followed our decorous saunter. It was dead boring for all concerned. A complete "grade A" waste of time, apart from some snide and jealous remarks from shipmates who had seen us "pull the birds." So ended the affair which never really began. With relief we bid them "goodbye" on the earliest returning Kirkwall Ferry, and made tracks for the nearest pint. The girls, no doubt, were also well pleased with the outcome.

As there was an obvious need to make one's own entertainment, and on the principle that "things only happen if you go out and make them happen", we used our spare off duty time, to kill time, to the best possible advantage. Gutter Sound is hardly the Solent, and Lyness bears no resemblance to "Cowes," apart from the flagpole in front of the F.O.I.C's offices and club house. Nevertheless, a few of us communications ratings thought it was about time to enjoy the thrill referred to as "messing about in boats" By Kenneth Graham of Wind in the Willows fame. Granted appropriate permission, we took away a ship's whaler equipped for rowing.

The wind was northerly, and cold, and it was altogether not a very good idea. Our excursion was therefore brief, and within a very short time, we were back at the ship's companionway, discharging our crews, before rowing the whaler to the lifting/recovery position alongside, below the falls. (Hoisting tackle). Unfortunately, I found everyone had gone, leaving me alone to pull this most awkward of boats into this position. Absurd of course, but we were signalmen (the intelligence brigade) not seamen. I manfully pulled on my oar. (You can only handle one at a time) and finally managed to achieve the objective, but at some bodily cost. I ruptured myself!

After several weeks of looking at this swelling in the private regions I reported sick. After not too long a period, I was transferred to the hospital ship "St. Julien" berthed in Long Hope. I was joined by an appendix case in the cot next to mine. Male sick berth attendants soon dispelled our dreams of pretty nursing sisters mopping our fearful brows whilst recuperating. Perhaps we would get some sick leave. There must be some perks after major surgery. We were surprised when without telling us aforetime, the "St. Julien" sailed. Even more surprised to learn that whilst at sea our operations would be carried out. Remembering the jibes that Naval surgeons only knew how to use knives and forks, we were not encouraged. Burials at sea, if mistakes happen, would be too convenient.

I was lucky. They did a good job and with stitches resembling laces on a football, I survived. "Appendix" wasn't so lucky. His operation, technically more simple than mine, was marred by unforeseen complications. Whilst unconscious on the operating table, a kidney dish containing the surgical instruments was lodged between his upper thigh area, to prevent it dislodging when the ship rolled. However, the dish had only recently been removed from the sterilization cabinet and was piping hot. It wasn't obvious to those gathered around and "Appendix" wasn't in any position to complain. The resultant scald burns were horrendous and his love life received a severe setback for several months. When you break a fingernail it seems to catch on everything.

We arrived at Aberdeen. There was no brass band playing *Anchors Away*. There was no cheering crowd to welcome home the wounded heroes of the home Destroyer squadron. An ambulance was alongside the quay gangway. We awaited the stretcher party. Instead a white robed moron disguised as a sick berth attendant, but behaving like Dr Kildare, ordered us out of our cots. Taking our personal knick-knacks with us. Thus clutching our stomachs to avoid shedding their contents on the fish dock, we made our over cautious way down the gangplank, into the boneshaker of an ambulance and into convalescence. After convalescence at a naval hospital we were glad to get back to active service, without sick leave. If you haven't got trouble when you enter a naval sick bay, you sure have by the time you leave!

On return to Scapa, we were glad to re-engage in our deep rut of time killing. A walk one dank afternoon took us far into the hillside behind Lyness. Turning for home however, we found ourselves at the wrong end of a small arms firing range, and practice was in progress. Away in the distance, prone figures lay horizontal between two poles, each flying a plain red flag. That we were in range and danger was evidenced by the noise of bullets cutting through the turfed peat all around us. Little cover was available. We ran in panic through bog, marsh, and stunted fern growth. Stacey lost both "wellies" doing a hop, skip, and a jump across a particularly soggy piece of terrain. We did not wait to render assistance - it was "devil take the hindmost!" Finally we crouched in the lee of a foot high bank, running alongside a sluggish burn. Here we stayed, until the red flags were hauled down, and once more gravitated towards the warmth of the fleet canteen.

To describe this as a canteen is stretching the imagination. It existed entirely for the consumption of beer. No spirits, just brown frothy liquid. I often sampled this, partly from the bravado of youth, because I did not wish to be the "odd one out," so called sociability. But I never really enjoyed it, or became addicted. Nevertheless, I confess to over-doing my capacity, on more than one occasion. One such event resulted in a couple of watches of Bunting Tossers, about eight of us pretending to be "ships of the line" responding to flag commands, like battleships on manoeuvres. Various patterns could be formed by ships linking together, or singly i.e. "line ahead" (one behind the other), or all simultaneously turning to port or starboard - into line abreast. The S.O. or leading ship would hoist flags "9" + blue pennant i.e. 90 degrees to starboard or port.

Immediately these flags e.g. Blue + "9" were wrenched down - the action was executed. All other ships repeated the same flag hoist to acknowledge that they had seen the instruction, and were ready to obey, when the moment came. If any ship did not understand the instruction it repeated the hoist, but held the flags halfway up "the halyard" at the dip. When ready, the flags were hauled close up. Thus eight sailors could be seen staggering and cavorting across a muddy football pitch, using the right arm well extended above the head to represent flags. A ragged, dishevelled and disgusting detachment. Various manoeuvres were performed from the F.S.B. (Fleet Signal Book) ending with the entire fleet falling headlong into a ditch.

Shipmates on *HMS Tyne*

Off duty time together

Bennett. McLeod, Bond, Bruce, Harper

49

Douglas (arrowed) with shipmates

Douglas Bruce and his shipmates aboard HMS Tyne in Scapa Flow

9

PETSAMO & KIRKENESS

The Russian convoys

Two separate staffs were accommodated on HMS Maidstone - one was the ship's company, the other was the Admiral's staff. The latter was a support staff to attach itself to wherever the Admiral Commanding Orkney Shetland (ACOS) decided to go, often at very short notice, and the members of the staff soon earned the tag `Death or Glory Boys'.

Try as I might, I had the greatest difficulty getting off the 'Death or Glory' list. During my time in exile at Scapa, I was unfortunate enough to catch up on temparary draft chits for destroyers on the Russian convoys - cumbersome, slow-moving, vulnerable assemblies of cargo vessels which took about a month to make the return trip from Britain to Murmansk or Archangel with supplies for the Russian forces. The home fleet, in theory, offered protection. Detachments or squadrons were usually sent in accompaniment. Each convoy was given an identity number, prefixed by the letters PQ when moving northwards and QP when returning homeward... Artic clothing was provided in the form of a hooded duffle, woollies and thick oiled-wool stockings. Other items, scarves and gloves were provided by one's relatives or the various home-base societies i.e. Red shield, Church Army, WI or simlar institutions. we were very glad of these home comforts.

A destroyer or escort screen surrounded each, and the naval squadron was usually just out of sight, but nearby. the threat of the german battle cruiser Tirpitz, lurking in Norwegian fjords was ever present... Packs of U-boats wrought havoc with these heavily laden vessels, packed to the gunwales with military supplies of every description to assist the Russian Armys and Air Force. long range bombers from occupied Norwegian air bases made life difficult on several occasions.

But beyond and above all the man-made difficulties was the weather.The cruelness of some of the storms beggars description - shrieking winds blowing horizontally across mountainous peaks and troughs of tornado-torn waves for day after day and cutting open exposed skin as if with razor blades, and ships of thousands of tons crashing through the crest of one liquid avalanche, to slide awkwardly down the green spume into the 'valley' only to be faced with yet another advancing hillside of water of savage magniture. It was terrifying to behold. Truly the sea can be cruel. my lasting impression was that its was far more frightening than anything the enemy could do. The little ships fared the worst in such conditions. Fuel oil maintained the balance acting as ballast, but on the long trips this needs topping up – clearly impossible refuel at sea under the conditions described above. The effect of this lack of stability often made destroyers roll to unbelievable angles. I was on watch when the chief engineer appeared on the compass platorm to plead with the skipper either increase speed or change course beacause there was a danger of rolling beyond our ability to recover. We were ordered to alter course!

Few meals could be cooked during such onslaughts; Snacks where taken by those with cast iron stomachs. my digestion never adjusted to this treatment. I lived on liquids for nearly seven days and then could only stomach toast. Rum, I firmly believe, kept me going. I have vivid memories of coming off watch, stumbling below, where my hammock was slung, swallowing my neat 'tot' almost in one gulp and eyes streaming from the thick rum fumes falling into bed. Where I finally felt the liquid get to work on my circulation, life returning to my toes, feet, then spread upwards via the limbs, body and finally into my head, eventually reaching the brain and sending me into a mercifully deep, alcohol-induced sleep. This was the only escape from the brutal reality of what was going on everywhere else.

They say the years blur the edges of your recollections, and that you only remember the pleasant experiences. Not true. The Russian expeditions were horrific. There was nothing heroic any of us did. We acted on orders, performed the duties for which we had been trained, and took our chances of surviving against the elements and enemy action. Many did not live to tell the tale, those that survived look back gratefully, but in horror.

When Maidstone's spell of duty came to an end I was transferred to HMS Tyne, a custom-built destroyer and a fine ship. As part of the admiral's staff, I was lent as temporary cover to the communications branch on several other ships. One was HMS Escapade, which I joined at such short notice that she was already under way, then the drifter taking me out to her drew along side

We were part of a squadron of seven sailing north to Iceland, sailing north to an Icelandic destination when there was a huge explosion, and one of the other members of the convoy, *HMS Echo* disppeared behind a huge cloud of spray. when she reappeared her whole forecastle had gone - only her bridge was upright and afloat. Immediatley some one on her signal staff flashed a message through the still falling spray 'MINED'. I often think of the courage and coolness that action took; whoever it was must have been in a terrible state of nerves. Many lives were lost.

30th July 1941

One afternoon, I was suddenly aroused from a rum soaked slumber and advised to get ready to join the Destroyer *Intrepid* within the hour. Hastily I started packing many things, bundling them into a kit bag, unstowing my hammock, and reported to the midship gangway. No one else seemed to be coming with me. I was to be on loan for "whatever." *Intrepid* was already preparing to slip away from her gutter sound mooring. *Tyne*'s motorboat conveyed me across to number 17 buoy.

Air Bombardment at Petsamo and Kirkeness

This trip turned out to be a long distance raid by members of the home fleet, on the twin towns of Petsamo and Kirkeness. These two towns, nearest to the most northern part of Norway, were to be disturbed by our attack. Two aircraft carriers, *HMS Victorious* and *HMS Furious*, plus a Destroyer screen, steamed hopefully unobserved past the north cape, and then southerly into the gulf leading to the towns. Just out of sight, the carriers turned into the wind, releasing about twenty Swordfish biplanes. These were out of date and nicknamed "Stringbags."

The bravery of those Fleet Air Arm pilots beggars description. They staggered off the flight decks, each loaded down with an standard but heavy torpedo and full petrol tanks. Forming up, the airborne squadrons headed off over the horizon. We waited with apprehension. Unobserved we may have been, but we were unlikely to remain undetected for much longer. We were about to "poke a stick into a hive of bees!" The waiting was nerve wracking.

On the ships R.T. (Radio Telephone) pilots' voices could be heard shouting and screaming whilst they carried out their attack on shipping, dock installations, warehouses and any military targets they could identify, with their torpedoes. After "milling around" in the gulf, the first Swordfish hove into view, and we turned into the wind to receive her. Slowly others started to return and seemed to take an age to land on again. Of those who flew off, 13 planes failed to return. The agonising decision of how long should the fleet "hang about like sitting ducks" had to be made. Some retaliation was bound to be mounted, and we were well within bomber range.

Night falls early in winter, in fact there is little daylight. For once this was a definite advantage for us. We were on our way home, but we were also a long, long way from "safe water." Everyone was secretly thinking "let's get the hell out of here!"

Fortunately a huge fog engulfed us as we steamed in single line ahead – for 2/3 days – and although very vulnerable, we were not discovered or attacked by German planes or sub. Scapa was safely reached. This was a poor result for such a dangerous plan.

HMS Escapade – Royal Navy Destroyer built in Greenock, Scotland. Commissioned in 1932

HMS Intrepid – Royal Navy I Class Destroyer built in Cowes, Isle of Wight. Involved in the pursuit of the Bismarck in 1941.

HMS Obedient – Royal Navy Destroyer built in Dumbarton, Scotland. Commissioned 1942.

HMS Tyne – Royal Navy Hecla Class Depot Ship. Commissioned in 1940.

10

HOME FLEET GOES SOUTH

After the first four and a half years of naval service, spent based mainly at Scapa and operations in northern Atlantic and arctic North Cape waters, it was with some surprise and not a little excitement, that our floating base went south. *HMS Tyne* was leaving her moorings and going to sea! Some said it was to avoid 'grounding' on the mountain of empty tin cans from the NAAFI and gash, from the cook's galley, which had accumulated below the ship's 'gash-chute', as she had swung around her buoy at Scapa! The explorers of the future will wonder, as they trace this precise circle of garbage, why and how? What caused this new phenomena? Some ancient ritual? Had it any relation to patterns cut in corn fields? The famous name of ship salvers Messrs Danks and Cox were still raising WWI German vessels from the Flow in Gutter Sound. Might they not find it more rewarding to start recycling thousands upon thousands of empty metal cans and ex corned beef containers?

Meanwhile, *Tyne* made her majestic way down the west coast of Scotland, through St George's channel and out into the wild Atlantic. She was a better sea boat than many a destroyer it had been my misfortune to be aboard, whilst accompanying the Rear Admiral Home fleet destroyers of the earlier years on his various excursions from Scapa, on some mission or other. *Tyne's* ship's company could now claim to be real sea-going sailors, heroes at last!

Off Lands End in very heavy weather, we were amazed to be confronted by a line of real, ocean-going "Fighting Ships,"(friendly ones) in 'line-ahead' formation, all careering south westerly away from the French coast! They made quite a sight, crashing through vicious waves and charging through those rough seas, each ship with 'a bone in its mouth.' Puzzled by this behaviour, we ploughed on, hugging the southern shores of Cornwall, Devon and Dorset. Finally we passed Poole and thence slipped quietly into the quiet Solent via the Needles, which is not the normal approach to this busy waterway. We did not know it, but it was just a few days before operation "Overlord", D-DAY!

We were told to anchor off Gilkicker Point, the local and nearest signal station. This position lies about halfway towards the Isle of Wight and commands a magnificent, grandstand view of the Solent. It was an unbelievable view of fantastic naval activity, as far as the eye could see up and down, including the whole of Southampton's dockland frontage, the Hamble outlet, and the rest of this huge stretch of sheltered inland waterway. Craft, vessels, tugs, boats, motor launches, jolly-boats, destroyers, scores of landing craft of all descriptions, drifters, capital ships, supply vessels, ferries. Ships of every type and then some we did not even know were ships; an endless panorama of shipping shapes of every size and sample. So *many* ships were gathered in this large reach. To try to look through them was like staring at a forest of trees without branches. The sea was black with masts and rigging. There was also an undeniable tension in the atmosphere. Something tremendous was about to happen.

Few German aircraft were evident. Much activity by the RAF and Yankee air support was going on continually, day and night. There was rocket-propelled V1 pilotless "flying bombs", giving some cause for concern and stories of people being chased through the dockyard by one out of control. They were as deadly as they were unwelcome, but posed no threat to the operation in hand and became common place events of each day, as though they were a shower of rain!

Visit to my brother Alan

I managed to get a permitted overnight shore leave pass until 11am of the following morning. My younger brother, Alan, was by now a new trainee for the Fleet Air Arm Photographic unit stationed at Bognor. I managed to travel there without let or hindrance, although now I cannot remember how I went, It must have been by train.

My naval rating these days was that of a Petty Officer, Yeoman of Signals. I was still wearing 'square rig' (blue collar with three white stripes, signifying Nelson's sea victories of Corunna, Nile and Trafalgar). A qualifying period of one year has to be served before being allowed to change into 'Fore & Aft' rig (peaked cap, navy blue doe-skinned suit, white shirt, stiff collar and black tie). I presented myself at 'Reception' (in naval terms this equates to coming aboard). I was quickly accepted, made welcome and shown very courteously into the Regulating Petty Officer's office. This made me think that they were not very used to being visited by seagoing matelotf!

Although I did not realise this fact at the time, my brother Alan was immediately found, summoned and wondered why he should be required to present himself "at the double" to the R.P.O's holy of holies. This normally could only mean "big trouble." Alan told me later of the reputation this particular P.O. had. When initially joining ship (arriving for training) at this rather quiet, off-the-beaten-track establishment, he was greeted as part of the new 'intake' by this all powerful gentleman, who announced slowly clearly and with great emphasis "You will find this place to be a very quiet little number. Not many of these will be found in 'the Andrew'. There is only one b***** snag with this establishment... and I am it!" In Gilbert & Sullivan's words he was truly 'in charge of the King's navy.'

Alan and I spent a very pleasant evening chatting about the last few years of separation from our family circle and general talk of the present state in which we found ourselves. The war had so far 'called' upon the services of our elder sister Norma, who was secretly engaged at Bletchley Park in Buckinghamshire. She was helping to break the German and other complicated codes. Subsequently, we now understand that many successes were achieved resulting from the enormously important secret information, being made available to our war time leaders. As we chatted on Bognor's prom, we pondered upon the use which was going to be made of several curiously shaped huge blocks of what looked like concrete, moored close in close to the shore line. They were part of the breakwater caissons used in the Mulberry Harbour operation and were about to be towed across to the Arromanches beachhead where they would be sunk into the framework of the artificial harbour. The Mulberry Harbour is acknowledged to be a very great reason for the successful outcome of Overlord. When the time came for my brother Alan to return to his 'stone frigate' of *HMS Daedalus* to continue his tuition, I had the late night task of returning to Portsmouth in time for catching my liberty boat at 1100 hours to *HMS TYNE* on the following day. This was a problem. Even in peacetime the S.R. Train frequency from Bognor via Chichester to Pompey is "sporadic." In wartime it was diabolical and after 2100h non-existent. Hence, a hitchhike was the only possibility. I walked to the very edge of town and stood beyond the barbed wire, which seemed to be rigged for some reason of hindrance. It seemed flimsy beyond all standards but it was there for some reason, if needed to seal off the back of the town. (It may stop a billy goat but not a tiger tank)

Shortly in the gathering gloom a dark green, army-type truck hove into view and stopped in response to my gestures of help required. It was very full of very full and merry Polish soldier lads returning to their camp, the location of which was "somewhere nearby" on the Chichester road. As this was also my destination and my main objective of reaching before nightfall, I joined and volunteered to assist the driver find the way home inside the driver's cab. My ulterior motive was to get myself as near to a railway station to Portsmouth as possible.

In a second hand beer haze we charged along the lovely country lanes, with much hilarious, tuneless singing and much foreign language - good or bad I do not know, but all of it very loud. I was dropped off in the middle of a very sleepy Chichester and pointed in the general direction in which I thought they should proceed. They disappeared into the night which had now fallen, it being well after 2300 hours. I really had no idea where they were going and in a restricted war zone during wartime you do not ask too many questions or directions. I sought out a police station to occupy a spare cell for the night. I soon found one that was open for business and presented myself (this was standard practise for servicemen road travellers). Not being drunk, dishevelled or disorderly, the duty P.C. took pity on me but 'just happened to know a couple' who would offer B&B. Throwing caution to the winds and 'any port in a storm', I accepted. The thought of staying in a hotel was foreign to me. Hotels were where Officers took Wrens!

The couple were decidedly odd! They stayed up all night to avoid being in bed when a doodle bug was dropped. I was in no mood to discuss the pros and cons of this line of thinking. I had no such reservations however, sleep was sleep and very precious in my eyes. It meant I had to share a double bed with some enormous snoring twit who snored at both ends! But beggars cannot be choosers.

After breakfast, about which I have no recollection, I recall standing on Chichester Station platform, with a small army of 'civvies', waiting to catch the 8.15 train to Pompey. I felt very unshaven, scruffy and ready to return to my ship, to get cleaned up and 'Bristol fashion' i.e. respectable again. This accomplished, I quickly settled back into the watch-keeping routine.

Ordinary Signalman Bruce
HMS Tyne 1943/44

Shipmates. HMS Tyne.

Shipmates. HMS Tyne. October/November 1943

HMS Tyne. King George visit. Scapa Flow. 15·55 April 1944.

HMS Tyne. Scapa Flow. 1943

King George VI is introduced to the crew of HMS Tyne on a visit to Scapa Flow in 1944.

11

D-DAY MEMOIRS

What a sight! What a wonderful moment of history and what a privilege to have this prize grandstand view of this most momentous and fantastic invasion operation ever mounted and never likely to be repeated. We did not even cheer the soldiers who passed slowly by our ship. What awaited them on their appointed landing beaches? What awaited them was too awful to contemplate.

Sailors not normally given to pray, paused, awed by the implication of events, to say a silent prayer for these, our companions in arms, gathered together from many different countries and backgrounds, to face and fight the greatest evil of the twentieth century. There were frequent reports which followed of daily progress and a heavy sigh of relief when several days later, all was said to be going better than had been expected.

HMS TYNE – Flagship for Home Fleet Destroyers stationed off Cowes Portsmouth.

One of the compensatory things of being an RN signal man was reading semaphore made with hand flags. This was especially so when the messages were sent by Wrens. They were, like all good signalmen, required to perch, with a good clear silhouette and raise arms straight and clear of head and body. This they did at the Solent Signal station on Gilkicker Point to very good effect. Needless to say, this was clearly a bonus. When these lovely creatures "reached for the skies", beneath their crisp white blouses, much else was refusing to stay static. Many a word of the text was 'missed', by those with one track minds. Talk about bouncing bombs! Life in the Solent was a thousand times more interesting than Gutter Sound had been in the Orkneys.

Craft of curious design and an even more curious purpose, floated by, driven under its own power. One was, for all the world liked a four legged table, turned upside down and slowly drifting along with its legs up in the air. This was another part of the Mulberry Harbour. When in position the legs would be lowered, disappear to rest on the seabed, leaving a floating platform to adjust itself, to whatever state of tide pertained. Another was a gigantic cotton reel, half above the water, the rest below the water line. This, we learned much later, was PLUTO (the Pipe Line Under The Ocean). This unique and fantastic invention, never before used in any conflict, allowed fuel to be pumped through it across on the seabed from England to France, thus transporting the millions of gallons of essential fuel for all mechanical purposes; tanks, cars, mobile guns, jeeps, lorries etc, an absolute necessity for the success of the invasion. The days passed quickly and events were overtaken by weather, which would always have an enormous bearing on the possible success or the unthinkable failure of operation Overlord.

D-Day Dawned – At Last

Finally, during the middle watch (midnight–till 4am) of 5th-6th June the colossal RAF and USAF flights of gliders, bombers and fighters took place - flying in droves overhead, noisily and apparently endlessly. We listened to R.T. messages filling the airways, spoken excitedly and tensely without understanding a single word. But from this very unusual breaking of radio silence we gathered that the assault on Hitler's Atlantic Wall was taking place. As dawn broke the radio news of the 'Para's' landing behind the beaches was broadcast by Ike (General Eisenhower).

From the high up vantage place of the flag deck of *HMS Tyne* we had a grandstand view. We looked down on the most tremendous sight imaginable, and never to be repeated. History in the making. Two by two and stationed side by side like a huge caterpillar track, stretched out along the whole surface of the Solent, LCTs and landing craft of every sort and description, were making their way from the landing/embarking 'hards' from all along Southampton water and elsewhere. They were passing in a never ending procession, below our mooring and out and beyond the Nab tower fortress, at the eastern approach to the Solent. As far as the eye could see, this unwinding coil of motorised ships, floats and boats made slow but very unsteady progress across the choppy channel towards France.

It was obvious to anyone moving about in this restricted area that something enormous was being planned and that we were part of it. After five years of hardship, bad news, defeat, regrouping and non-progress the morale level was now building, the troops finding something to believe in and the probability of actually winning the war was well within our grasp. It was exciting to be part of it!

As is well known now, the whole part of Southern England had become a huge ammunition and supply dump. Tanks, landing craft, aeroplanes stores of all sorts, shells all the catalogue of war making paraphernalia was under wraps, hidden in forests, camouflaged in deserted fields. It choked roads, tracks, and farmland. This was all scheduled to back up our armies and be moved in support of them to France. Much of it would be moved via the aforementioned Mulberry Harbour... when the time came.

12

SAVERNACK

Last days of "embarkation leave" late 1944

Running up to and during this wartime period, the whole of the South Coast of England was a restricted zone (an area encompassing Bristol to the west, Cambridge to the east, and everything below a line drawn between the two cities) and had been steadily being filled up and stockpiled with all the thousands of things necessary for D-day (June 1944) – tanks, petrol cans, food rations, war materials of every kind. All the local aerodromes were full of parachutists in training for the Battle of Arnhem (September 1944). Gliders were being flown in mock trials and hundreds of paratroops were being dropped out of planes. We were not close enough to know whether those whose parachutes unfortunately did not bounce when they hit the deck! The operation was a complete shambles, costing thousands of our forces lives.

After the excitement of "Overlord" some unexpected, but very welcome shore leave was granted. We did not realise that this 'leave' would be our last in the UK for many months to come. It was given to those now to be drafted out to the Pacific zone of the Japanese war. You do not ask questions (you do not get the opportunity anyway). You just get your gear ready and yourself, to catch the first Liberty boat heading for the shore!

My now wife, Joan (wed 8th March 1942), had been evacuated to live in a safer area when she was preparing to deliver our first child Robert Douglas Bruce. With her grandmother of advanced age, she was staying in a very beautiful and picturesque cottage in Great Bedwyn, Wiltshire. This was and still is a delightfully peaceful place not far from Marlborough Hospital, where she was 'booked in', when her time came (25th March 1943). Although Great Bedwyn is not particularly well known and could be termed, 'situated at the back of beyond', it is on the Great Western main railway line of Paddington to Bristol. Often during day and night through the miniscule wooden railway platform, would flash noisy, fast expresses, carrying bored-looking passengers to their destinations, heaven knows where.

This lovely 'chocolate box' home was called "Far End". So called, for in those days it stood quietly serene with its tiny front garden and thatched roof with green fields stretching for miles behind, the last building of any sort at the far end of the lane it fronted. It was part of a small village community overlooking the Kennet canal, which ran alongside the railway line. It was offered for sale by the owner, a Mrs Corns, for £200! Today's value would be perhaps £200,000 or more! We missed our opportunity to buy.

Some distance away to the North, much noise broke out from time to time. This originated from huge Yankee and British air force aerodromes. I have no idea what they were called - *in those days you did not ask questions!* They were practising hard, towing gliders tied behind them. We watched them dropping hundreds of parachutists, who fell to earth well away out of our vision. This was a strictly 'restricted' war zone area. Training was in full swing for the forthcoming assault on Arnhem, where disaster awaited this over-ambitious operation later that year.

Walks were often taken along the canal bank or railway line to Little Bedwyn, where Joan's cousin Pamela Goldsack lived with her parents, Aunt Florrie and her husband "Guggie", who ran a home for twelve blind inmates. This home was called The White House. Pam was about twelve years old. She was very slight build and had lovely long fair hair, long legs and a charming personality despite being an only child. She still remembers those far-off 'Far End days'. They certainly are still very poignantly treasured in my memory.

I suffer badly from hay fever. This dates back to my childhood. It was almost unbearable. From the age of ten at a boarding school in Kent for four years this was terrible inconvenience. Crawling through wild field grass some two feet tall was the start. It stayed with me for several years after that. Country life was not popular with me. Strangely once at sea, away for a full twelve months, the complaint almost left me and stayed dormant for many years into my adult life to follow. During these lovely rambles we watched poor chaps going head first out of the side of their troop-carrying planes. Many crashes were involved. White nylon parachutes filled the skies like mushrooms, but some sadly did not always open... the learning curve had a big cost attached to it.

Finally, the last day of leave taking arrived. It was planned that Joan and I would walk from Great Bedwyn to Marlborough Station through the Savernack Forest on our way. This walk is filled with poignant memories. The forest was choked with the paraphernalia of war. Huge pyramids of shells, stacked like cans of beans in a supermarket; rows and rows of ammunition boxes; vast areas of parked tanks, jeeps, wheelbarrows, legs, wooden planks; stores of all description. It was all so out of keeping with the natural beauty of this wonderful wood. No-one appeared to be on guard or to challenge us, so we two lovers strolled along together, taking was what likely to be our last walk for months, maybe years, or perhaps even forever!

This sentiment so played on my mind that I felt I had to write a poem, trying to express or capture our feelings, the atmosphere and poignancy of this quality time together. It went as follows:

Savernack

The saddest day in all my ken

Was one in bleak October when,

With cheeks so flushed and hair blown back,

I left a girl at Savernack.

Throughout the leave the dread prevailed,

The separation date – I failed

To push it from me, hold it back –

Soon we must part at Savernack.

Through countryside when Autumn's grip

Was slowly strangling drip by drip

And changing all from green to black

That day I left from Savernack.

We strolled along, linked arm through arm;

The air was crisp with faint alarm,

For soon we'd part. Our lives would lack

The warmth of love at Savernack.

Each, deep in thought, content in heart;

The years ahead soon each would start,

An empty useless routine track

'Til once again at Savernack.

Like withered leaf upon stark bough,

Clinging to life - life we knew now

Too soon would fall the axe and hack

Last loving ties at Savernack.

She looked so lovely at my side;

Our son at home, my other pride;

So much, so much was I to lack

To end of life at Savernack.

Her azure eyes were crystal clear,

Her smile was warm, her forced-back tear

Across my heart a ghastly crack.

I'd leave all this at Savernack.

We tramped through lanes, the woods, a farm,

Her chilled hand in my glowing palm;

No words we needed to complete,

The harmony of each heart beat.

But talk we did of no import,

Of daily things, the earthly sort

While in higher plain thoughts did commune,

Conscious of what would come too soon.

But, reassuring each one's mind

That nowhere else could either find

Happiness that knows no bounds;

This love 'pon which the cynic frowns.

This force which no-one comprehends,

That strikes a chord and music sends

Throughout a day of dull routine

A symphony of notes that seem

To blend each word, each thought, each deed;

To be loved and loving far exceed

The drab and drear materialist,

To whom such things do not exist.

Oh, freedom from this earthly rot

In love thou hast, without hast not;

This power compelling to adore

This lovely girl still more, still more.

If she but knew – but then, she must;

How utterly she has my trust,

Though years of loneliness ensue

Love will remain in me, in you.

So now, as to the station nigh,

Our time, our thoughts, have fluttered by;

We gazed, with horrified ghostly stare

At cold steel rails so shiny, where

With angry roar and hissing steam

A juggernaut came to crush our theme,

To stamp and rave, obliterate

Our tenderness with snorts of hate.

Last fleeting glance. Last touch of hand.

The Farewell Kiss, we understand.

And getting in, I threw my pack

And through the window, gazing back;

The dim outline, along the track,

My wife – the girl I left at Savernack.

This was penned in the Autumn of 1944 before being sent overseas, and before Ann, our second child, was born in August 1945.

My first camel sighted 1944

Port Said -Entry into the bitter lakes

Port Said

HMS Tyne makes its way down the Suez Canal

13

GOING FOREIGN

The British Pacific Fleet Goes Foreign

We sailed as part of the above force, known as "The Train." This Americanism meant that part of the mobile backup force which was necessary to keep a fleet at sea. We had most of the logistical equipment to support ships away from any base. All ships carried armaments of sorts although we were not regarded as "Fighting Ships of the Line!" Thus *HMS Tyne* sailed for foreign waters, for the first time in her history.

What was more important to me was that I was also, and for the first time, "Ship's Company." I was no longer on the Admiral's Staff. I had recently passed exams at Rochester/Chatham and was upgraded in rating from Leading Signalman (Hookie) to Acting Petty Officer. For a whole year I must continue to wear "Square Rig," as opposed to "Fore and Aft" (Peak cap, collar and tie). But on my arm I proudly displayed "Cross Anchors," signifying that I rated as a non-commissioned officer. I was a full member of the ship's company, in my own right.

I moved into the P.O.'s mess and I now qualified to take my rum ration 'neat.' In the change I was also qualified "Yeoman of Signals." This pleased me because I had worked really hard to pass the very stiff exams. For the six weeks at Chatham I worked with another chap who wanted desperately to get through. No leave was taken, even though it was easier to reach London than from other depots. Together we concentrated on the one objective: passing. Night after night we would revise and put one another through the day's lessons. Constantly revising and making it a serious business of committing to memory what we needed to know. It was tough, but it was also worthwhile. Once through, I began to enjoy, almost for the first time, my days in the Navy. A new respect was afforded you both by ratings and more senior ranks. Yeoman of the Signals to this day are still regarded well by the Royal Navy.

The journey through the Mediterranean was uneventful. From memory there were about nine ships in our formation. Stations were taken up in three columns, the *Tyne* serving as the leading ship of the column to Starboard of the Commodore flying his flag in the "General Mann" (American). Time has erased the other names, but I believe we were accompanied by the *Moultan*, as leader of the far left column and somewhere in the convoy we sailed with "*The Dominion Monarch.*" As a matter of pride we made it important to be the slickest ships in the whole bunch to repeat the Flag Signals hoisted by the Commodore. Our job was to copy whatever signal he made and hit the blocks at the masthead first. It was good fun and broke the monotony of the voyage. We slipped by Malta, a vague, misty island hidden from us by low cloud.

Port Said - Aden

The morning dawned brilliantly over our arrival at Port Said in northern Egypt. As we approached, the harbour gate to the port was just about to open. Penned up inside were scores of gaily-coloured sails of fishing dhows waiting to pass out and begin their day's fishing in the Med. It was a very spectacular sight. One by one the ships of our convoy entered the port to learn that it was blocked half way down, by someone running into the bank! Midday finally saw us being allowed to follow on.

The Canal was nothing but a very large ditch, which had been dug by the sweat of thousands through sand from one end to the other. No hills were visible. It was flat, arid, sun-baked, dry and very uninteresting. During the forenoon, a short time of shore leave was granted and I purchased a very cheap pair of 'leather' sandals. These were fashioned from camel hide and fell apart the first time they came into contact with water! A very short time ashore found a group of us having our photo taken by our first encounter with an Egyptian street "snap shooter". We, being good ambassadors for our country and a little cautious and suspicious, kept hold of him by his collar, until we saw the photos were actually being developed! As soon as we paid him he disappeared!

About half way along the canal opens out into three large lakes, known as "The Bitter Lakes" for what reason I know not. No one, in their right mind ,would ever be mad enough to drink water in such a place. We passed a huge British transit camp. No one thumbed a lift! It was rumoured that this spot was a favourite of King Farouk (who was still around at this time). Here, we were told, he would flout his enormous obese body, helped by Nubian bronzed young ladies, whilst playfully splashing in the waters!

Late starting, we were late in arriving at Suez, well past midnight. We 'dropped our hook' at an allotted berthing area, to await daybreak. The action of our anchor hitting the seabed stirred up years of the foulest smell I have ever encountered. Someone likened it to the odour of all the combined sewers of Christendom being opened at the same time. Being pitch dark we fell asleep with this nauseating atmosphere pervading everything inside and outside. In this part of the world, there is always a lack of really clean cooling fresh air and it gets worse as you sail down towards Aden.

At Aden the following day *HMS Tyne* made an awful job of berthing. The ship's rope handlers were very new to sailing about the seven seas and thus lacked expertise when it came to handling ropes! Eventually we got tied up alongside the jetty and a run ashore was planned. A group of us hired an Arab boy who was in charge of his taxi, although he only looked about twelve years old. He was very good on the horn but not so competent on the gears. We crashed along noisily and he drove us down a narrow street with Arabs smoking bubble pipes in every small open-fronted veranda. We were surrounded by men in Middle Eastern head dress - Keffiyeh - and in flowing white robes, which reached down to their ankles. They were almost inside the open topped car which was moving far too slowly for my liking.

We were through the town and on our way up the nearby mountains, where there were wonderful water reservoirs, or so we were led to believe. These were natural reserves of fresh drinking water and supplied the whole area. Having taken in this sight it became obvious that our young driver had a fixed idea that the next stop would be a brothel. It so happened that his sister ran one! None of us had the slightest intention of falling for this suggestion so with a clenched fist in his face, we were delivered back aboard. We sailed for Ceylon in the early morning.

Run ashore. Port Said. End of 1944

Ismalia - Approximatley half way down the Suez Canal

14

CEYLON AND ON

Aden - Colombo

Having refuelled at Aden, which is reputed to be one of the hottest places on this planet, we set sail for India and Colombo in Ceylon (now called Sri Lanka). The trip was very uneventful. The ocean was friendly, but very localised sudden patches of bad wet weather were encountered en route. They were real tropical short-lived downpours of squally rain thrown down by the angels of weather in bucketfuls. At least they afforded you some breaths of fresh air in the sultry heat at sea. Flying fish accompanied us alongside both bows but otherwise there was little to get excited about. By now my skin had taken on a very marked tan, except where it mattered most!

My only recollection of Colombo was that it was overcrowded with throngs of local chaps, fully clad in white night shirts reaching down to the ground over which they appeared to glide noiselessly, as though they moved along on castors, instead of feet! Bare feet make little sound on the sandy covered tracks they called roads. As you walked along, a million bright tiny little fire flies glittered in the dusky night air.

Trincomalee

This famous port is now to a jaded and gilded memory as close to paradise as any earthly place on earth. A perfect harbour and a perfect climate. Situated half way down the eastern seaboard of the Island of Ceylon (now Sri Lanka) it was used as a forward base in support of the far eastern war, being conducted by thousand of our troops in Burma and Indonesia. It was too far away to be ideal for that purpose, but those of us who were privileged enough to spend time here will never forget its wonderful ambience.

We made the most of our surroundings by taking the ship's small sailing boats away for a whole day or an afternoon. We knew we could always rely on a gentle zephyr which they call a monsoon. It started to blow from the same direction every day at 6am and lasted until 6pm without fail. You could therefore, plot your sailing course long before getting into the boat.

Swimming was perfectly safe, behind shark nets and the water was azure and warm.

Whilst swimming one afternoon we were shaken by an explosion. It occurred as we were swimming towards a somewhat tatty raft made from large disused petrol cans tied together. The sensation was likened in my imagination to being narrowly missed by a slimy tentacle which whipped close to me enough to drive the air out of my lungs. I panicked and swam like mad for the raft. I recall the flat top of the raft sloped down at one corner, almost under the water. I shot up this ramp like a spent torpedo! The others as they arrived also wondered what had caused this experience. The explanation lay in the fact that a motor torpedo boat well outside the boom had dropped a depth charge and the shock waves had been felt by us in the water some two/three miles away!

Sailing days

Sailing the ship's 'whalers' became an off duty delight. Even though the whaler is, of all sailing craft, the most awful boat ever invented to sail. Heavy, cumbersome, ugly to look at and non-responsive were its natural characterises. Nevertheless, it was a challenge and turned long empty afternoons from boredom into fun. As I was known to love sailing and had had several turns at borrowing the ship's boats for this purpose I was the obvious choice to be appointed by our Signal Bosun as coxswain of the Communication's team in the inevitable interdepartmental Divisions regatta. Only prestige was at stake, no cup or money were involved.

A pre-set race plot was arranged and each day the Divisions of the ship's departments raced against each other. Then our day arrived! I made a complete "dog's breakfast" of the whole affair. It was the most embarrassing day of my life.

My crew were "bleary eyed and zombie-like after drinking their grog and stumbled into the whaler so late that we did not get underway in the time allotted and were thus disqualified, even before the starter's gun had been fired!

Our whaler refused to catch the wind and was swept along the ship's side bouncing off every rivet and obstacle imaginable. Both our small masts (main and mizzen) passed under the wire supports, which hold the forward boom in place at right angles to the ship's side. We were inextricably trapped! A very difficult situation from which to extricate oneself, even if an accomplished and experienced mariner, which was far from describing my own capability. The ship's side was lined with leering, cheering, leering catcalling foul-mouthed matelows. Scorn was hurled down upon us from a great height. You felt even the seagulls were enjoying a belly laugh at our predicament.

"Bombhead" (as he was known) our Commander, a most feared gentleman, was purple with pent-up rage. What had the Navy become, when it numbered such grossly unsuitable candidates amongst its crew, who were behaving like fugitives from a Laurel and Hardy film plot. It was an absolute disgraceful exhibition of appalling ineptitude. Bombhead dispatched a 'three badger' down to set us free (which entailed unshipping both masts) We were then to be taken round the course set whilst our opposition was out of sight! We were late home for tea that day and few had the cheek to show their faces in the signalman's mess!

Another memory from Trinco was the fire-fighting course carried out on shore. Trust the Navy, it was 102 degrees in the shade but drills went on, which required you to enter a burning shack constructed from corrugated iron sheeting over which petrol had been thrown and you had to navigate to safety up a 'shougly'(wobbly and unstable) steel ladder wearing protective clothing and a gas mask! Good fun in Iceland but not in the tropics! It was here that a reminder of home happened quite by accident. I had the good fortune to have a dalliance with a local Wren. Carol was a colonel's daughter and was earlier in Scapa, when I was serving aboard the Maidstone. She had been transferred to Ceylon and was the person who passed us one of the first messages we received on our arrival. You will recall that signals always had to be authenticated by the sender stating their name at the end of the message. She had enquired had I been at Scapa etc. The result was that she agreed to meet me for coffee, at the local coffee place known as the Elephant House (there are very few elephants in Ceylon).

Abroad, WRENS were Officer-Only property and did not normally mix with riffraff or ordinary sailors no matter how well mannered and well spoken they happened to be. Carol made me an exception to the golden rule. The Wren and I were very obviously an unusual sight in these circumstances, as we were to find out from our friends later on. We enjoyed our coffee and chatted, recalling those now far-off days of tele-flirting with the girls during the night watches at Scapa. We were always trying to shock the girls by loose talk whenever the opportunity presented itself and they were as much to blame as we! Both sides felt they could let their hair down a bit because they were safe so to do without losing their self-respect or virginity. Often the whole night watch would sing and serenade these luscious creatures with their siren voices.

Whilst seated at wrought iron tables with chairs at decorously placed intervals, not too close yet not too far, a sudden interruption shook us both. A loud 'WAAAAMP' noise coincided with an enormous husk, still encasing its coconut, falling between us making quite a dent in the soft undersoil! A tree rat had gnawed through the stem and released this heavy load to crash earthwards. It was probably my closest shave with death during the whole war! I paid the bill and left Carol without any feeling of guilt although my name stunk in the nostrils of honest men for days.

Bruce and Baker sailing in Trincomalee

15

"GINGER" BANKS

The diversity of human personality never fails to amaze me. In the gathering together of a bunch of people from every walk of life, it is therefore inevitable that some stand out in the memory for one reason or another. The reason for recalling "Ginger" Banks (why ginger? He had red hair), was his unfailing propensity for becoming involved in one calamity after another. A sort of chain reaction of minor disasters, a gentle Jonah.

Ginger was a "short service" rating, sucked in by conscription, trained/ processed at Skegness, and thrown in at the deep end. A nice sort of lad, but in the rough and tumble, was oddly out of time. If there were problems it was a safe bet that Ginger would be, if not the cause, certainly implicated. Thus, to have Ginger, as one of the watch (team) was a guaranteed liability. He was "U.S." as the derogatory term implies, useless. They tell us that everyone has a redeeming feature. In Ginger's case, it was exceedingly difficult to discover even the smallest trace of such a feature.

My recollections of him begin while crossing the Indian Ocean. Having just suffered the outrageous humid condition, and breathless atmosphere of the Red Sea, Suez, and Aden - we sailed those beautiful blue waters with some relief - especially the sudden squalls and (very) sudden downpours of torrential and refreshing rain. There was very little warning of these "showers," and although the rain was warm, it was still penetratingly wet. Ginger was the junior hand of the watch. His duties were to fetch and carry, to make sure senior hands were constantly supplied with tea, cocoa or cold lime drinks. He was a "Gofer' (go for this, go for that).

At sea, the *Tyne* had the luxury of two cabins located on the Flag Deck (Immediately under the bridge) which were designated for the use of the navigator and captain, while at sea. They were small but very comfy, and more important, situated immediately opposite a heavy armour-plated door which gained access to the charthouse. Naturally, this was the nerve centre of the ship. Charts were spread out in good artificial light on wide chart tables, equipped with all the paraphernalia of navigation instruments to hand. At night, strict blackout was always a priority at sea. Thus when the sliding door was opened, it broke the electrical circuit controlling the power and the lighting, to avoid anyone forgetting to switch off before opening the sliding door. All the doors on this deck leading to the signal house, to the gun shelters and the two cabins, already mentioned, had this arrangement.

The navigator always liked to be called ten minutes before any alteration of course was made, thus his "call" had become part of Ginger's watch responsibilities. However, the sultry conditions plus the apparent lull between rain showers, tempted the "navvy" to take his folding canvas bed out to the extreme wing of the flag deck where he had bedded down, behind the heavy metal casement of the Oerlikon gun turret, having given firm instructions to be called at the appropriate time.

A sudden torrential downpour hit the deck about an hour later. No one remembered to call the Navigator. He was drenched and his mood can be imagined as he strode up to Ginger, ordering him to collect his now sodden camp bed, which now had pools of collected rain water and resembled a giant sea slug. Ginger proceeded to collect the bed from the port wing and trundled with it to the charthouse door, through which the "Navvy" had just disappeared. "Off" went the lights inside, and Ginger, plus bed, blundered in. When the metal door shut and the charthouse was again flooded with light, the still dripping wet Navigator exploded with rage. "Not in here you b******g fool. Take it to my sea cabin opposite!" Anxious to avoid witnessing an apoplectic fit, Ginger complied. "Off" went the light again, as he backed out into the midnight blue of the Indian Ocean, leaving oaths of hatred floating on the heavy air, until cut short as the armour plated door slid back into its closed position. A pool of water on the chartroom floor bore witness to Ginger's recent visit.

Into the sea cabin opposite, Ginger went. After closing the wooden door he tried the light switch. Nothing happened. So he lent the sodden camp bed up against the cabin wall bulkhead, which happened to be fitted with an electric fire. Ginger closed the door, and carried on with his middle watch duties. Two junior signalmen chatting around the back of the flag deck noticed smoke issuing from the square port of the Navigator's sea cabin. Gazing in, they could make out the glowing red embers of the canvas bed - now on fire inside. Panic shouts of "Fire!" and much scurrying about ensued. Plus sand, and water hoses being thrown in every direction, before the charred skeleton, the remains of a wire framed camp bed was declared to be: "no longer a hazard" - and was thrown overboard.

"Commander's Report" was the seat of justice and punishment, and Ginger Banks was duly sentenced some days later, when the *Tyne* was at anchor in Colombo Harbour. The sentence passed on Ginger was extra duties (in his normal spare time i.e. off watch or standby). He was required to spend time and an hour hosing down the forward forecastle: he, and another defaulter.

So, on a lovely sunny morning, Ginger and his mate "drew" the necessary equipment i.e. hard long handled brushes, fixed up the deck-coupling to the hose, switched on the pump and started to spray the sun kissed deck with salt water, starting just behind "A" gun turret. What came out of the hose had to be pushed and brushed around, to reach every corner of dry deck and then any excess to requirements 'over the ship's side'. Not a very difficult task one would think. But nothing was ever very difficult until Ginger got his hands on it! Under the almost disinterested gaze of the duty PO, they performed in Laurel and Hardy fashion and everything appeared to be hunky dory.

Unbeknown to Banks however, was that the TR4 forward transmitting wireless station square port, normally closed, was on this very day... open wide! Inside P.O. Tel Wiggy Bennett was running a routine operations test on this vastly expensive equipment which required the place to have maximum ventilation. These tests could only be carried out at special intervals and whilst in port. They were very powerful transmitters and generated a great deal of heat. They were caged and protected by close mesh steel metal netting housings.

Our two defaulters were by now well into their tasks, out of sight around the corner and whistling away pretending to be almost enjoying the exercise! They were totally unaware that their hose, being somewhat old and suspect, had developed a 'kink' and twisted slightly, increasing pressure in the folds. The more they dragged it along, the greater the pressure. Under normal conditions it would not have mattered very much, if a jet of salt water had spouted in an arc of 5/6 feet, as it would have fallen harmlessly back onto the already wetted deck. However this hose kink happened just below the open window of the now sweltering transmitter room of the TR4 station. Thus the jet speed up and right through the opening and straight on to the humming machinery.

Sparks and blue electrical flashes resulted. Fuses were blown throughout our entire wireless communication resources, and the risk of serious fire caused panic. One of *HMS Tyne*'s jobs was to be a never-shut ear to the Admiralty who controlled our activities even at remote distances. Day and night we had to keep in touch. Thanks to Ginger and his mate that was not now the case and no one knew what the extent of damage was or how long it would take to get it sorted! OR IF IT WAS PERMANENT!!

I cannot remember if Ginger was ever acquainted with the havoc he had wrought. He and his mate were well away from the scene by the time investigations began. Many months later Ginger was drafted to aid the Americans. We were in Leyte Gulf in the Philippines. He seemed pleased, almost honoured, when our boss, the Signal Bosun told him he had been 'volunteered' to man a signal station, located about seven miles away from our anchorage. Through our telescopes it looked like a deserted hut or 'bird hide' built just above, on a ledge leading to the water's edge.

Ginger was seen swimming and gambling about at the foot of this structure making it impossible to "raise him" on an Aldis lamp, to pass any messages. You could call until you were blue in the face, but he was enjoying his ice cream and pop too much to be bothered with the war! Sadly we heard months later that Ginger had been killed. Allowed a short relief 'leave' he was a passenger in a Dakota, which crashed, without survivors. Ginger maintained his reputation as a living disaster - right to the end!

Field Marshal Montgomery visited HMS Tyne as the vessel sailed from the Solent to the Far East.

Field Marshal Montgomery onboard HMS Tyne

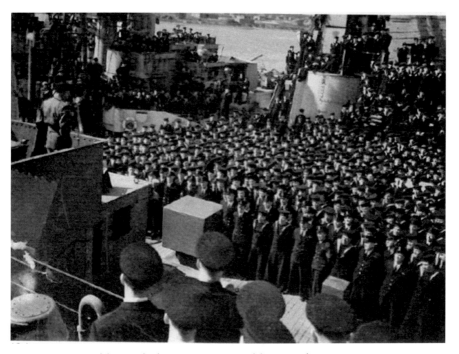

Field Marshal Montgomery addresses the crew

Crossing the Equator

16

SHOOTING FOR THE STARS

VIP visit

One bright and sunny morning a visit was paid by Admiral Lord Louis Mountbatten. He was in supreme command of the whole show for far Eastern activities. He gave us a very good upbeat pep talk yet down to sea level message. No promises were made. Soon we were to set sail into the real war zone i.e. The Pacific.

Ceylon to Perth and Freemantle

This was a delightful cruise with many unusual weather features along the route. Probably the most bizarre was when *HMS Tyne* tried to shoot down a star! It was whilst on passage between Ceylon and Australia. There had been reports of aerial missiles. Explosive devices held up by helium gas balloons, which dropped after thousands of miles with devastating results. The sighting of a very bright shiny silver object made during the forenoon watch was sufficient to send all the ship's company to "Action Stations". When all guns crew were 'closed up' (ready for firing) the range of shot was the next and very puzzling consideration. Here was a dilemma. Fortunately the cruiser that was accompanying us, noticed *HMS Tyne* getting excited about this mysterious object and tactfully mentioned that this star had also given them the same scare once before! All crews were immediately "stood down." and our attention was redirected, to the normal ceremony of "Crossing the Line". The equator was duly crossed and the proclamation issued was dated 29th January 1945.

Freemantle welcomed us with open arms. Every member of the ship's company received a gift of goodies, consisting of beautiful fresh fruit, chocolates, nuts, and tinned everything. Mine contained a tinned Christmas Pudding! These gifts were organised and donated by the ladies of the equivalent of our W.I. They were appreciated enormously. Fresh fruit had become an absolute luxury.

Sydney early 1944

Sydney is not called the world's most wonderful harbour for no good reason. It was and is the most fantastic city, port and seaside resort all rolled into one. The shelter provided by the Heads (entry) is remarkable and absolutely perfect for any amount of worldwide shipping. On either side are stretches of golden beaches stretching for hundreds of miles both north and south. One of these is called Manley which is of world renown. The terminal point for the inner harbour ferries from Circular Quay. Across a very short strand lies Bondi Beach. This really is some place. It is world famous for surfing, with the most huge rollers always pounding in upon the firm sandy shore line. If you want sea shore it is here, *big time*.

Once inside the Heads it is twelve miles to the very centre of town. Striding across joining North & South stands the one and only Sydney Harbour Bridge. Affectionately known as "the coat hanger" carries traffic in several lanes through a toll and holds the whole place together. I stand in awe of this massive construction although man-made, in its original vision, size and grandeur it is truly magnificent. The harbour consists of several bays most heavily forested, both large and small which team with life. House's chalets, cottages, jetties, landing places, huts' strips of beach and sandy coves, make up the landscape, reaching up the hillsides that form the horizon. Small foot passenger ferries 'dot' back and forth endlessly day and night. Most originate from Circular Quay and are very, very cheap, providing some terrific views of the town suburbs.

After five years of rationing clothes and food, everything, even the more basic utility had long since disappeared from UK shops. The contrast of Sydney made an enormous impression on me and I am sure it would again if I was ever fortunate enough to revisit it. As we strolled away up hill from Circular Quay, we Walked up one of the main city streets passing more and more shops in the Macquery Street area, groaning with goodies to eat, drink or wear. The pavement vents filled your nostrils with temptation. Huge steaks were being fried before your very eyes in some shop windows. No coupons were needed, just large appetites! Huge department stores hove into view. It was a dazzling experience. The luxury of sitting down to tackle half an animal fried with onions, tomatoes etc was irresistible. Jewellery was on show and could be sent home. And of course... the girls!!

Sydney had everything a sailor could desire - plus a whole heap more. Only some of which can be recorded here for decency sake! It is an understatement to say the girls looked bronzed, healthy and exceptionally attractive. Good figures well dressed and all looking for partners. This legacy was from the influence of the previous visits of the US fleet. Relationships were easily formed. Dating was a double edged affair. You were picked up whether you were aware of it or not. The local main attraction for local talent was the dance hall - way up the top end of main street hill. Now demolished but I believe it was called the TROCADERO. Hundreds of boys met hundreds of girls here!

Bennett and Douglas Bruce. Sydney. 1945

Bondi Beach, Sydney

17

SYDNEY BEHIND US

It was early 1945.

We understood that we had a spell of "working up" i.e. getting to know the ship and we would be hanging about in Sydney for about twenty-one days. So we tried (very successfully) to make the most of it! It did not take us long to rent a flat onshore to act as a base for our activities. Wiggy Bennett was my run ashore mate. He was a Telegraphist Petty Officer and completely free lance, a very laid back character if there was such a thing. He and I got ourselves measured up for brand new P.O.'s rig. I cannot remember the huge store where we bought this beautiful doe skin cloth but it was expensive and this very obvious when wearing it. We knew we were the 'bees knees'!! Thus with a base to explore loads of action going on around us we went to discover the wild life in the concrete jungle surrounding us.

So much now is lost in a misty mire of so-called merriment, flavoured with memories of outrageous adventures all over the town from Bondi Beach to Rushcutters Bay, to the end of the local railway line out towards the Paramatta River on the north side of Sydney. On leaving harbour to join the war effort shooting practise drill was necessary. I had seldom heard *Tyne*'s guns fired. A shooting practice was arranged and took place. A small civil type plane towing a drogue target many yards behind him flew alongside *HMS Tyne* at a suitable height. We opened fire! Immediately distress calls were received from the pilot, which on being separated from the Aussie language said, "I am pulling this target... not pushing it!" It was his lucky day... he's the one who got away!

Farewell to Sydney and a long sail northward began towards New Guinea to a temporary base behind coral reefs off a place called Manus. This is part of the group of 'offshore' scattered islands which make up the Admiralty Islands. In themselves they were of no significance except that they still had Japanese people hiding on them, who were being left to starve, whilst the main US thrust, moved towards invading mainland Japan. Before this could happen several battles still lay ahead. One was the capture of Luzon and Leyte in the

Philippines.

The British fleet was not welcomed generally by the Americans. They did not want anyone to steal their thunder or be able to make any claims that they could not do it on their own. Nevertheless the British Pacific fleet was of considerable size, over 800 ships of all wartime description, very experienced and battle tried. Plenty of skill, good seamanship and courage was available for the asking and Churchill was determined to have some part in the final defeat of the Japanese. The British fleet was needed where the action was.

Japan was in its last desperate throes: an enemy fighting every inch of ground with huge losses (on both sides) at sea and on land. Most of the large naval battles were history by the time we arrived on the scene and we were very pleased about this. Thousands had been killed as the Yanks pressed on from one island to the next, regardless of causalities. But it was far from over yet. If ever anyone doubted that the dropping of the atom bomb was justified, to bring sanity back to life, they should understand the cost that had been paid largely by the Americans up to this point in the war. Millions more would have been killed if we had not had this decisive weapon.

View of Sydney Harbour Bridge from Taronga Park

Sydney Harbour Bridge

Taronga Park

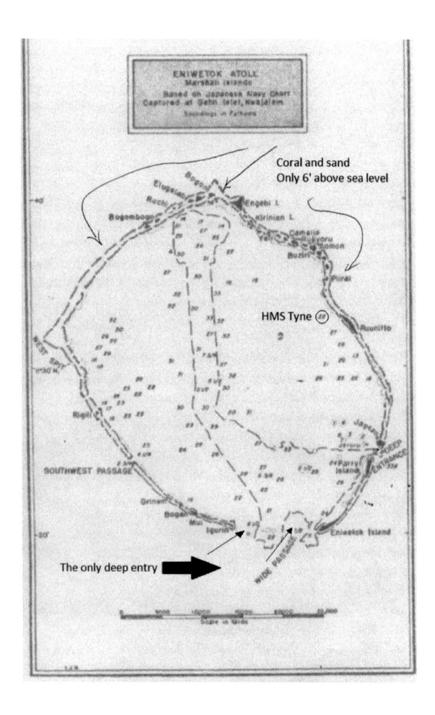

18

ENIWETOK

Marshall Islands June 1945

A thousand miles from anywhere! A thousand miles from nowhere! (that's more or less the original of the native name for this deserted atoll in mid -Pacific). This is a place that is as far away from anywhere as you can imagine. You have to spend about five days to sail to it. When you arrive, the first thing you see is a huddle of masts all apparently stationary, as though at anchor, in the middle of one vast empty never ending horizon of sea. Our radio picked up the identifiable sounds of the Yankee programme called Duffle-Bag. This was popular with mostly Glen Miller type music being played. We were occasionally lured by the slinky voice of Tokyo Rose, Japan's ruse-like Lord Haw Haw, to undermine morale.

The US Navy had fought bitterly over this staging point in their determination to hop skip across the wideness of the Pacific Ocean. Over 350 marines lost their lives before securing the place and took the lives of 2677 Japanese who defended it. It had no real airport potential being the remains of an extinct volcano. There are numerous uninhabited isles and islands around and some were occupied by some Japanese. They were left to starve as the war front passed over their heads. Only the very old top of the volcano remains. Thus the rim forms a huge oval azure coloured lake, miles across, kept in place by sand dunes, with no point higher than about ten feet above ocean level. This outer crust was surrounded by coral reefs over which the mighty Pacific rollers endlessly vent their wrath, with crashing white foaming waves. The entrance was narrow and only possible at the right time of tide.

Our ship drew 26 feet and therefore had to use the deepest approach point to avoid going aground. I have good cause to remember our arrival as I was nearly demoted for my action as Yeoman of the watch! There are times when everything seems to happen at the same moment. At such times the words of Rudyard Kipling are most appropriate... "If you can keep your head when all others about you are losing theirs..." This was such a time for me. I was the one who almost lost the place and later, when on Captain's report, was fortunate not to lose all my naval rating seniority, respect, reputation, achievements and possibly any pension rights and other benefits, if found guilty "as charged". This occurred when entering this isolated spot.

As Yeoman of the watch I was responsible for answering and receiving a host of pent up messages awaiting my ship's arrival. These came as flashing lamps, aimed at your bridge, from other ships, the harbour-master's tower or control point, C in C's aboard the fleet's flagship, tugs, and pilot's boat. They indicated where we were to anchor, tie up or berth, pick up a pilot (if we needed one), other pressing, urgent, tactical signals i.e. sailing instructions, for forward orders and priorities such as hospital casualties etc. It was the signalman's job to read and report these ASAP to the officer of the watch, on the compass platform and to get his prompt reply back to the originator. Hence four or more lamps would be flickering directly at you at the same time, from various different directions. It was a time of hectic activity. It was also unavoidable. It meant efficient, alertness and competence (for which we had been well trained) to cope during several stressful minutes.

In anticipation, each signal watch of four individuals would be doubled up by the added presence of our opposite numbered watch, (making eight signal personnel) on the flag deck, in readiness to accept any messages that were thrown at us "immediately, if not sooner!" The flag deck was thus manned by double the normal number of us, each ready to read the identifying call made to us on up to four lamps, both large and small. Each ship has a number and ours was F23 . This is our 'E-mail identification' our ship's pennant numbers. This method is still in use today. This call was repeatedly made by flashing light at the ship until you answer it. Nowadays, with Morse no longer used, I suppose they text one another! (in between watching the cricket!).

Thus there is considerable activity on occasions, but it only looks like chaos, to those not attuned to differentiate, whether you are being called or not and whether you are in the middle of taking down a message being sent. Some messages were not necessarily aimed at you but the ship behind you! Amid the flashing chaos it was difficult to see which group of two signalmen were actually reading which set of flashings, but the main occupation was to ensure that anyone who was calling us was indeed being answered and read. To the untrained it would appear to be exceedingly baffling. Most officers were supposed to be able to read the Morse code, but in practice very few did and others who thought they were fluent, had difficulty in recognising S.O.S. In the midst of this and whilst coping well, the Captain (for whom I had the greatest respect) called out, "Yeoman! Answer that call off the port bow!" It so happened that I had been reading this light for at least five minutes if not longer. My answer should have been "Aye Aye Sir", or, "Thank you. Sir." But I regret to say my answer was "Aye Aye Sir, I am already reading him!"

It was not the words but the tone of voice used to deliver them, which caused the trouble. It so happened that Commander "Bomb head" (our dreaded mentor, reputed to be the illegitimate son of the Witch of Endor) had arrived on the upper Bridge and had overheard this interchange. He thought my answer to the skipper smacked of impertinence and I was put on a charge of "insolence to a superior officer." This was serious and it was also untrue. I was called to give an explanation by my immediate boss, Signal Bosun, the Warrant Officer in the Communication's Division. The following day I was 'on report' and stood accused, in front of the Commander. He was a real terror. An arrogant, loud, awesome, apparently raised from birth in Captain Bligh's character- no one ever escaped. His word was law. Somehow, however I did escape the punishment I may have deserved. My friendly Bosun acting as my advocate had worked a miracle of mercy. I was reprimanded and warned but found "not guilty." It was the nearest thing!

So Eniwetok, my memory of you in that far-off spot, in the middle of nowhere, holds no fear, but I hope that when I stand in front of the Judgement Seat of heaven it will not be Ex Commander Bombhead, late of *HMS Tyne*, who is on "offenders duty" that day!

My final recall is of taking a whaler full of naked Petty Officers ashore, swimming and fishing for loofah sponge which was growing wild like seaweed, along the shoreline, just below the surface, and of lying in gorgeous sunshine and watching the shadows of very small insect-like spiders, run over the sand. You could only note their shadows when they moved, they were so small and darted about so quickly.

Eniwetok Naked Swim
June 1944

This chart is based on one captured from the Japanese and shows the Eniwetok Atoll, 1000 miles from anywhere.

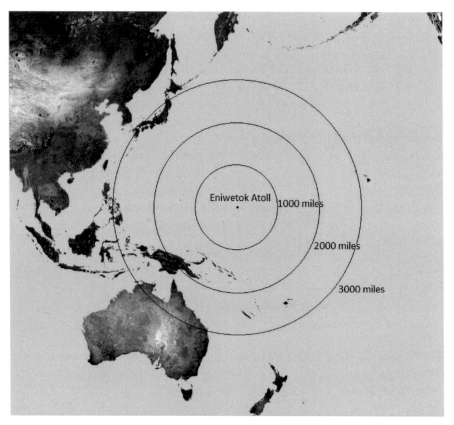

Eniwetok Atoll – In the middle of nowhere

19

THE END IN SIGHT

Manus was in the tropical Island group lying off the northern shore of Papua New Guinea. Here my naval career was taking shape towards its fulfilment and end.

World events which were about to take place were so horrendous that it is well that only a few had any prior knowledge. I recall musing with my opposite number and shore-going pal Wiggy Bennett (he was our ship's Wireless Telegraphist of Petty Officer rate), one evening after supper as we lent over the ship's rail, which we often did when putting the world aright! It was obvious something was going on which we couldn't quite understand. Wiggy remarked that there was a very unusual "hush" going on in his world of radio telegraphy. It was absurdly quiet.

Secret signals had been received, that wireless traffic was to be kept to an absolute minimum, to leave the airways free from congestion. There was to be "no batting the breeze!" WHY? What could be so important, that such a decree had had to be issued from both the Admiralty in London, (to whom we had always to maintain a 'listening' ear) and the American network directed from Washington, which normally pumped out an endless stream of incomprehensible garbage.

Tension was beginning to build up again. It was like this just before D Day. But the Pacific circumstances were so vastly different. Huge naval battles had taken their place in the pages of recent history. The Yanks had played a colossal part, bled and died using the strategy of leap-frogging from island to island, atol to atol, across the wide Pacific Ocean. They landed on each significant place a token force, large enough to subdue any opposition, to maintain the captured objective, before passing on eastwards towards the final objective of the Japanese homeland itself.

I feel it is necessary here to recap the whole landscape of this far eastern campaign. The main sea battles were fought out long before the British Pacific Fleet arrived in the area. The giant, stung into murderous activity, by the shock, humiliation, treachery and defeat of Pearl Harbour, was now wide awake and taking a truly terrible revenge. The venom of the American counter attack was genuinely awesome.

The first major victory saw the sinking of four huge aircraft carriers from which the Japanese fleet never really recovered. This was the battle for Midway Island situated to the North of Hawaii. These carriers were part of the Japanese task force which had damaged Pearl Harbour so badly. Thus June 4th 1942 was the very beginning of the end of enemy sea supremacy. Two huge and brutal sea fights were early in February 1942 - the Java Sea and again the Coral Sea on the 8th May. At this point the U.S. Navy was probably at its weakest strength after losing so many capital ships in Hawaii and generally being so ill prepared for wholesale hostilities.

Eniwetok was the next to fall (Feb 1944) after over two thousand Japanese were killed at a cost of 300 US Marines. This atol was pounded to pieces, by heavy naval gunfire before the Marines went in. These battles were unlike any sea battles ever conducted before. The opposing fleets were not in sight of one another, Bombers flew over the distant horizons, to attack and return to floating platforms, far removed, from the scenes of action. The relentless drive eastward went on and Leyte Gulf, Iowajima, and finally Okinawa followed. Hundreds of thousands of causalities in fanatical, blood curdling and ungentlemanly tactics on both sides. It was unleashed carnage on a massive scale.

Diary Entries - From other naval personnel

"HMS FORMIDABLE

Hit by Kamikaze suicide raiders, during the heaviest attack ever made on the British Pacific Fleet (BPF). This was on V.E. Day April 1945. A crashed Japanese plane, pierced the deck and burnt out a score or more aircraft parked in the upper hanger, also setting the hanger alight. Later the same day, *Formidable* sustained another hit "AFT" which reduced her speed to 7 knots. Meanwhile, her own aircraft were airbourne, waiting to "land on", when the flight deck had been cleared of wreckage, to receive them.

Formidable refused offers of help from other carriers in company, continuing to land her own planes and managed to get them all safely aboard and tucked away.

A truly remarkable piece of work. It is impossible to find words to describe the absolute fury, confusion, noise, explosions and complicated chaos that filled the skies and sea on every hand."

"From other ships, *Formidable* could not be seen for the terrific clouds of black smoke which enveloped her. These suicide planes and pilots always, repeat always, attacked the "carriers". Battle ships, cruisers, and destroyers were left alone apart from machine gun and cannon strafing. The "flat tops" bore the brunt of the war at sea in the Pacific. Each of the five British Pacific big fleet aircraft carriers were hit in turn before the end of the hostilities. None were ever put out of action or commission for longer than a matter of a few hours. Fires were put out and wreckage shovelled over the side, to remain in continuous fleet action. Attacks at the height of Japanese desperation, were from first light dawning until dusk. This was the daily experience for the crews of these magnificent ships."

It so happens that the author has, by sheer coincidence, been a neighbour to a surviver of this encounter with the Kami Kazi.
Mr Gordon Scott MBE has his own story to tell of this terrible incident, as he attended to the wounded, dead and dying in the "sick Bay" of HMS Formidable, now blazing on fire... What an experience!
Gordon and I have stood side by side, each Remembrance Sunday in Rothesay Cemetery for the last twenty three years!
It has been our pleasure and privilege to call to mind with enormous pride many names of the previous shipmates who died, in order that we may enjoy FREEDOM to be present on such occasions.

I return to the musing of Wiggy and myself hanging over the ship's rail. Here we were riding at anchor, still within sight of many Japanese soldiers in hiding up in the surrounding jungle vegetation and being left to starve to death, in this humid environment. This place is reputed to be the wettest place on earth, with 132 inches per year at Madang, just down the road. When it rains it seems like half of the annual rainfall falls within the first ten minutes! The Admiralty Islands were suitably placed as a base from which strikes could be launched at mainland Japan. Suicide Kamikaze pilots of the Japanese airforce were being used with terrifying effect on ships, carriers and battleships, HMS

Formidable being one of those. It was difficult to understand what huge strategy could be used to terminate the possibility of enormous casualties which lay ahead. The Japanese mainland would be defended fanatically to the last man and woman. You will recall the mass suicides, when the whole population ran and jumped off the cliffs on the Island Tinian. It became known that they possessed over 3350 KK planes backed by 5000 young pilots in training, to fly into targets of all descriptions. They had already lost 2500 of them in combat.

Whilst England was celebrating VE day a particularly vicious attack by Kamikazes was taking place which involved many of our ships and carriers, but not HMS Tyne. Even when playing with dodgems at the fair, it is difficult to avoid some mad one whose one aim is to destroy you. Oerlikon (very fast repeating cannon shooting guns) were mounted each side of the flag deck and we signalmen had been trained to use them. Each cartridge of shells held 60 canon shells. When fired these sent a trail of red tracer behind. They were wonderful to fire, really exhilarating. My efforts (fortunately not used very often) had earlier been summed up by our gunnery officer as "excellent directional fire but hopeless timing control". You were supposed to fire, short bursts, but in the thrill of action, it was impossible for me to pause and thus I 'let fly' and the whole was a terrific thrill as this noisy "she-bang" went up in great style. It was a great gun to use but expensive on bullets!

As our musing went on so did the drive towards the end of the war.

SUDDENLY THE BOMB WAS DROPPED.

Hiroshima and then 72 hours later Nagasaki. The pros and cons have been and will be debated for ever. To serving war weary folk whether in the services or not, they brought hostilities finally after six enormously stressful years to a close and stopped the further loss of a million more Japanese, American and British lives. The war was over and we could live at home at peace at last. The day we dreamed of had at last arrived. I do not remember VE day but I certainly recall VJ day. Evil had been defeated and the whole world was FREE again.

The Surrender was signed by Major General Umekichi Okada on behalf of the Southern Japanese forces on the 13th September 1945. The document of surrender was signed on *HMS Indomitable* in Hong Kong. The Yanks are not known for being backward in coming forward. Just as England had been saved by Errol Flynn, it was US "big shots" who all claimed to be the conquering heroes and had enough medals to prove it. Little acknowledgement of the part played by the BPF (British Pacific Fleet, one of the largest fleets assembled by the Royal Navy) was ever mentioned. General MacArthur (Commander and Chief of the US Army Forces in the Pacific) was 'signing for the world' in Tokyo. The Mighty Mac had returned and had hundreds of cameras (and medals) to prove it!

Looking for the foe

Signing of the Japanese agreement

Victory Parade
Hong Kong

DOUGLAS BRUCE served in the Royal Navy on board six different ships between 1939 and 1945 – first as a Capacity Decoder, then as an Ordinary Signalman, Leading Signalman and Yeoman of Signals.

20

THE PASSAGE HOME

The day had come. My naval career was almost at its end. Together with many hundreds of sailors, civil servants, ex Japanese prisoners of war, army and naval personnel, our course was set for Portsmouth, England and discharge from His Majesty's Forces.

The ship chosen for this sad but happy voyage was the ocean going and famous aircraft carrier HMS Indomitable, with her Paying Off Pennant (a long piece of bunting attached to the masthead, marking the end of the ship's commission) trailing out behind, helped with a few helium filled balloons. As we slowly got under way and the huge Sydney Harbour Bridge (known as the Coat Hanger) slipped further and further behind ships hooted, the marine band played *Take me back to dear old Blighty* – folk waved and sailing vessels lowered their club pennants in salute. Sydney's famous entrance was passed and now in the past.

The trip lasted some 8 weeks. This meant our arrival at some southern railway jetty would be just before the end of 1945. Stops along the way were made at Freemantle, Colombo, Suez, Port Said and Gibralta. Not a lot happened and the mood aboard was relief that the war was won, no danger lay below from 'U' boats and the things flying were friendly. Our POW's were from Changi and other Japanese hell holes and were in a pretty poor state of health. They were not a pretty sight and when exercising on the flight deck all personnel were kept out of their sight and were not permitted to speak, or look at them.

Slowly our homeward passage seemed almost boring. We followed a plotted course which did not allow many ports of call. Leaving Sydney we sailed westward through the Great Australian Bite. I do not remember docking at Perth before we set course for Colombo in what was then called Ceylon - a slight deviation took within clear sighting of the Cocos Islands. The wreck of the WWI German Emden still lay strewn across the coral reef when she was finally finished off by the Royal Navy at the end of 1918. She had given untold trouble during her activities against allied merchant shipping in the 1914-1918 era.

My recall of Colombo is one of colossal thunderstorms with rain 'like stair rods' - straight up-and-down stuff, which fell with the evil intent of smashing everything flat. At the time I was off watch and gazing with my hand out of the petty officer's mess porthole. Not a drop of rain hit me. The carrier's deck overhung the ship side V-shaped, thus the perpendicular rain fell far short of my spy hole. Commander Bombhead of *Tyne* would have been very cross. He used to employ a Petty Officer to patrol the upper deck "on leaving harbour". The P.O. was there to clout anyone 'hanging out' of any port hole- with a very large 'Nags head' (a rope end weaved into a deadly hammer head).

Pressing through Suez northward, a cloud of dust was seen at a huge camp on the Port Side - this turned out to be hundreds of soldiers running to wave to us, and begging a lift home! At Gibraltar several of us went ashore to buy bananas. Three huge thongs of green bananas were thus purchased and left at the dock entrance for taking aboard when we returned from our visit to more interesting places ashore. I have never seen so many pubs cheek by jowl anywhere else in the world, although they do say the Cut at Malta was also 'similarly blessed'!

I never enjoyed alcohol, believe it or not. It never got its hooks into me, although I always enjoyed my neat rum ration. Beer was frankly brown stuff that just didn't appeal. But I do have a love of onions. And there is no onion to rival a Spanish onion. Its mildness and flavour is unique. The locals were cute, the way they persuaded you to eat onions 'free of charge' - because they made you very thirsty as well! We staggered along the dockside, each with a large banana thong on our backs, reaching almost down to our ankles. On board the thing was broken into sizeable bunches and sold, still very green, to ripen up and be gloriously ready to eat three days later on arrival at Portsmouth.

Casting Off – Homeward Bound

Leaving Woolamoo Wharf

HMS Indomitable – Modified Royal Navy Illustrious Class Aircraft Carrier. Launched 1940

Farewell Sydney!

Final Thoughts

WHAT DID YOU DO IN THE WAR, GRANDAD?

This project was started more than sixty years ago "ever since when", my brother, Alan, has nagged me to 'get it down on paper' and my dear wife Isobel, 'to complete something I have started!'

The reasoning behind my brother's thoughts are that most **served** at some time in the forces, but it is unusual nowadays to find those, who due to the accident of birth, were destined to serve for the full allotted term of hostilities....i.e. from beginning to end. "The real Full Monty!" This privilege was mine.

On the day war broke out, our family, like millions of others had just heard Neville Chamberlain declare that we were now at war with Germany. "A state of war exists..." He had said. Many will remember that very shortly after that statement had been made, the first air raid sirens of war sounded.

We all took shelter... nothing happened!

As almost adults, we asked my Dad "What does a state of war mean Dad?"

He replied, many things which are not good news, that it will break this family up. We are bound to get separated.

His prediction was so right. Twelve months on, my eldest sister joined the Womens Auxiliary Air Force (WAAF) and served at the secret decoding centre at Bletchley Park. Even to her death in 1986 we never knew what she was doing. She had been sworn to secrecy.

My brother, Alan, four/five years my junior was training pilots in air combat with photography in South Africa before returning to serve on the home front, as a Naval Fleet Air Arm photographer. He it was who has continually encouraged me to write my story. So blame him for this book!

I am also so very grateful to have enjoyed the love, patience and encouragement of my wife Isobel, my proof reader (she can spell!) whom I married after the death of my first and precious wife Joan in 1987.

As the reader ploughs through the narrative, there should be evidence of a mellowing and maturing tone in the writing. A lessening of arrogance and gormless wit, together with less non-ecclesiastical anti-establishmentarianism of the rebel within. No doubt this was associated with the ageing process. The influence of experiences; of living to the riper age of tolerance, understanding and wisdom, especially once the barrier of becoming 92 is passed.

In retrospect there seem to be parallels to that classic Hollywood film "Forest Gump". Gump seems to pop up at many of the major important dates in America's WWII history.

In my case, these would be listed as Dunkirk, Russian Convoys, and Battle of the Atlantic; sinking of *HMS Hood*, Chasing the *Bismarck*, D-Day, and Pacific war-fare after Pearl Harbour, KAMI KAZI...and the dropping of ATOM Bombs on Hiroshima and Nagasaki.

"I was there or very close by..... Somewhere!"

When a boy reaches his late teens, the world becomes his oyster. He is past his teenage aggression and thinks he knows everything about everything.

Hence when I became 18, I should have left school, obtained a lifelong career with prospects, reached sexual maturity, formed some standards of behaviour becoming of a gentleman, become interested in girls and ready to begin life in the 'big' world.

Instead I was called up for the Royal Navy! (I had joined the RNVR in 1938).

Within less than three weeks (on 21st September 1939) of war being declared, I was called for Active Service.

My narrative, based on a faulty and failing memory, old photographs, previous non-Christian standards, never previously attempted to be put down on paper; is for no good reason, other than personal gratification, to see if it can be done. I hope this account has been of interest to some, being an account of my impressions and at times very biased observations.

I hope, by setting down some of my thoughts, reminiscences, impressions and experiences, garnished with a little humour, I have provided an enjoyable read. Certainly I have enjoyed the writing, as these incidents flash across the screen of my memory bank. My memory has played tricks, blunted the im-agination and blurred events, but this is not intended to be a war history, rather a reminder of what it was really like for those who served in the war.

In biological terms the six years between the ages of 18 and 24 should have been the best of my life. Maybe they were not so bad - after all, I had lived to tell the tale. I was just an ordinary lad, of ordinary background, class and ability, suddenly confronted with extraordinary, world-changing circumstances.Fortunately I came to an unshakeable faith in 1955, since when I have embraced the strongest of Christian beliefs, witnessing and serving the Lord Jesus Christ as one of His most unlikely but most ardent disciples.

The facts I have written are therefore believed to be true, and while I may have exaggerated on occasion to highlight the point being made, the basic truth is being retold - to the best of my questionable ability.

So the story ends with the sailing home to England from Australia. The cold grey arrival at South Railway Jetty, Portsmouth. 'Goodbyes' to fellow shipmates, many of whom were also leaving "The Andrew" for good (or worse), being thrown up on the beach like unwanted jetsam, to begin a new life in civvy street. War-weary but totally untrained for peace.

There was no lump in my throat as I sauntered through the dockyard archway for the last time. I was processed through the depot and equipped with 'civilian dress' (but I had looked smarter in my Petty Officer's doeskin. Not uniform, but made to measure in Sydney about a year previously).

I made my way home to my wife Joan, newly born daughter Ann, now a year old, and Robert my first born. What a wonderful family to return to! I yet had to face some sombre facts. Uncertain, unknown but peaceful days stretched towards the distance. The future held some promise – there lay hope and new adventure, so full speed ahead. I had joined the navy and seen the world or a very large part of it. Now I had to build a career and feed my loved ones adequately, to bring joy, security, and above all love to these very precious possessions. I had survived... thousands had not. Many were my 'late' friends.

World War II Timeline

1939

-   Hitler invades Poland on 1st September. Britain and France declare war on Germany two days later.

1940

-   Rationing starts in the UK

-   German 'Blitzkrieg' overwhelms Belgium, Holland and France.

-   Churchill becomes Prime Minister of Britain.

-   British Expeditionary Force evacuated from Dunkirk.

-   British victory in the Battle of Britain forces Hitler to postpone invasion plans.

1941

-   Hitler begins Operation Barbarossa – the invasion of Russia.

-   The Blitz continues against Britain's major cities.

-   Allies take Tobruk in North Africa and resist German attacks.

-   Japan attacks Pearl Harbour and the US enters the war.

1942

-   Germany suffers setbacks at Stalingrad and El Alamein.

-   Singapore falls to the Japanese in February – around 25,000 prisoners are taken.

-   In June, American naval victory at the Battle of Midway marks turning point in the Pacific war.

-   Mass murder of Jewish people at Auschwitz begins.

1943

- Surrender at Stalingrad marks Germany's first major defeat.

- Allied victory in North Africa enables invasion of Italy to be launched.

- Italy surrenders but Germany takes over the battle.

- British and Indian forces fight the Japanese in Burma.

1944

- Allies land at Anzio and bomb monastery at Monte Cassino.

- Soviet offensive gathers pace in Eastern Europe.

- 6th June. D-Day. The Allied invasion of France. Paris is liberated in August.

- September. Battle of Arnhem.

- Guam liberated by the US Okinawa and Iwo Jima bombed.

1945

- Auschwitz liberated by Soviet troops.

- Russians reach Berlin. Hitler commits suicide and Germany surrenders on 7th May.

- 8th May: VE Day.

- Truman becomes president of the US on Roosevelt's death and Attlee replaces Churchill.

- After atomic bombs are dropped on Hiroshima and Nagasaki, Japan surrenders on 14th August. VJ Day.

Glossary of Naval Terms

Blighty	A British slang term for Britain
Bunting Tosser	Signalman
Crashing the bonce	Sleeping
Crusher	Regulation Petty Officer
Grog	Genuine Jamaican Rum (Nelsons Blood)
Hooky	A sailor with anchor emblems on the arms or the uniform (hooks). Commonly used to refer to a Leading Seaman.
HO	Rating for hostilities only
Matelot	French for sailor
Middlewatch	A watch stood from midnight (0000h) until 4.00 am (0400h)
Plonkie	Name for boy sailor friend
Pompey	Portsmouth
Oerlikon Gun Turret	Naval revolver gun system
Rose Cottage	Sick Bay (Clinic)
Square port	Window
Tannoy	Brand name, commonly used term for a public address or speaker system.
Ullage skip	Lifeboat
Watch Keeper	Sets the hours of duty

Acknowledgements

My thanks to my brother Alan for spending time encouraging me to think back over my six year wartime Naval career and arrange my "jottings" into some kind of legible order he began the huge task of typing up my notes. He also has enabled this "dream" to become a reality and I am enormously grateful to him.

I have appreciated the patient promptings too of my daughter Ann, son David, his wife Sara and grandchildren to complete the work of compiling my memoirs. Special thanks to my eldest grandson, David, who reignited my interest again in 2011, when the family gave me a scratch-built model of *HMS Tyne* for my 90th birthday. The model had been completed by David, after the sudden death of his father, Malcolm, who started it sometime before.

Grateful thanks to granddaughter, Sarah, for her initial proof reading, editing and re-typing of the documents. Thanks also to Matt Meaney for the long hours he spent converting the chapters into digital format.

Thank you Jean and Shirley McArthur for all your help and expertise in typing and to Courtney Hobbs (plasticcloud.co.uk) for his cover art work.

Thanks to you again Alan and Ann for your long patience in the final stages in proof reading, checking and correcting which has been invaluable in improving the written text.

Lastly and by no means least, my thanks go to the patient support and encouragement of my lovely second wife Isobel, after the death of Joan in 1987.
I take these fleeting moments to find words that express my appreciation of all the love I have known from dear Isobel who has so enriched and filled my life. What a partnership! Wonderful on earth but perfected in heaven's place prepared for us by Jesus our Saviour.

HMS TYNE model made by Malcolm (son-in-law) and David Alexander (grandson) and presented to me on my 90th Birthday.

Naval Career Summary
WW2

Name........   Arthur Douglas BRUCE
Rating Petty Officer   YEOMAN OF SIGNALS
Service Number   LD9DX5232.
RECORD   for wartime active service.
Joined   RNVR in 1938.
Called up   21st September 1939 (H.M.S. President,
                            London.)
Joining routine   HMS VICTORY Portsmouth.
Discharged   End December 1945 (Group 11)

During my service I had terms of service aboard the following ships:-
HMS. CANTON - Armed Merchant Cruiser - Capacity Decoder. HMS
MAIDSTONE - Submarine depot ship - Ordinary Signalman
HMS TYNE - Destroyer depot ship - Leading Signalmen

Transferred to Admiral's staff Rear Admiral Destroyers Home Fleet.
Qualified and up rated to Petty Officer - YEOMAN OF SIGNALS
Whilst based at Scapa saw action when on temporary loan for special
operations to:-
HMS ESCAPADE
HMS INTREPID
HMS OBEDIENT

Transferred to "Ship's company" when HMS TYNE went foreign as
part of the British Pacific Fleet in 1944. Served in following zones :
Burma coastal water's based at Trincomalee Ceylon. Eniwetok,Bikini in
Marshall & Gilbert Islands.Australian home waters, Phillipines, Leyte
Gulf, Admiralty Islands
HMS Indomitable.   (Homeward passage and demobilisation)
Discharged 31.12.45.
Campaign Medals;- Atlantic, Pacific, Burma Star, Other medals , War
service 1939-45 (SPAM!) National Service
Long Service RNVR..